Indonesia Commission: Peace and Progress in Papua

Report of an Independent Commission
Sponsored by the Council on Foreign Relations
Center for Preventive Action

D1522511

Dennis C. Blair, Chair
David L. Phillips, Project Director

The Council on Foreign Relations is dedicated to increasing America's understanding of the world and contributing ideas to U.S. foreign policy. The Council accomplishes this mainly by promoting constructive debates and discussions, clarifying world issues, and publishing *Foreign Affairs*, the leading journal on global issues. The Council is host to the widest possible range of views, but an advocate of none, though its research fellows and Independent Task Forces do take policy positions.

THE COUNCIL TAKES NO INSTITUTIONAL POSITION ON POLICY ISSUES AND HAS NO AFFILIATION WITH THE U.S. GOVERNMENT. ALL STATEMENTS OF FACT AND EXPRESSIONS OF OPINION CONTAINED IN ANY OF ITS PUBLICATIONS ARE THE SOLE RESPONSIBILITY OF THE AUTHOR OR AUTHORS.

The Council will sponsor an Independent Commission when (1) an issue of current and critical importance to U.S. foreign policy arises, and (2) it seems that a group diverse in backgrounds and perspectives may, nonetheless, be able to reach a meaningful consensus on a policy through private and nonpartisan deliberations. Typically, a Commission meets between two and five times over a brief period to ensure the relevance of its work.

Upon reaching a conclusion, a Commission issues a report, and the Council publishes its text and posts it on the Council website. Commission reports can take three forms: (1) a strong and meaningful policy consensus, with Commission members endorsing the general policy thrust and judgments reached by the group, though not necessarily every finding and recommendation; (2) a report stating the various policy positions, each as sharply and fairly as possible; or (3) a "Chairman's Report," where Commission members who agree with the Chairman's report may associate themselves with it, while those who disagree may submit dissenting statements. Upon reaching a conclusion, a Commission may also ask individuals who were not members of the Commission to associate themselves with the Commission report to enhance its impact. All Commission reports "benchmark" their findings against current administration policy in order to make explicit areas of agreement and disagreement. The Commission is solely responsible for its report. The Council takes no institutional position.

For further information about the Council or this Commission, please write the Council on Foreign Relations, 58 East 68th Street, New York, NY 10021, or call the Director of Communications at (212) 434-9400. Visit our website at www.cfr.org.

CONTENTS

FOREWORD

After September 11 and the bombing of a nightclub in Bali, Indonesian authorities are showing new vigor in dealing with their country's pressing security, economic, and political problems. Indonesia's president, Megawati Sukarnoputri, is addressing difficulties inherited from the past. The economy has bounced back from its low point during the Asian financial crisis of 1997–98. The government has adopted measures decentralizing power and making officials more accountable. In addition, Indonesia has prosecuted Islamic fundamentalists involved with terror.

Despite this progress, Indonesia still faces a plethora of ethnic and religious conflicts. Separatist violence exists from Aceh, the westernmost province on the tip of northern Sumatra, to the archipelago's Far East in Papua (formerly Irian Jaya), where pro-independence groups have waged a long struggle against the central government.

The Council on Foreign Relations' Center for Preventive Action (CPA) works to develop and promote tangible, practical recommendations for averting deadly violence. The CPA's independent Indonesia Commission believes that the only way to avoid continued conflict in Papua is to give the province greater self-governance and a stake in the development of its vast natural resource wealth. The Commission believes that achieving sustainable peace in Papua would build momentum to address other conflicts across Indonesia, and that Papua could serve as a model for nation-wide conflict prevention.

The Commission argues that the key to peace and progress in Papua is the immediate implementation of the Special Autonomy Law, enacted by Indonesian authorities in 2001, but never put into force. The Commission's report offers concrete steps international stakeholders can take to encourage full and effective implementation of Special Autonomy. The Commission believes power-sharing represents a win–win situation by allowing the people of Papua to exercise full democratic rights as part of a unified Indonesian state. Failure to end the conflict in Papua could cause a spiral of deadly violence that would destabilize Indonesia. Nobody wants an escalation of conflict in Papua to result in a military crackdown and demand for international humanitarian intervention.

To increase incentives for Jakarta and Papua, the Commission highlights the history of close cooperation between international organizations and Indonesian authorities. The Commission proposes that the United Nations Development Programme (UNDP) launch a "Preventive Development Program." New grants for activities linking traditional development with conflict prevention would be raised via the World Bank Consultative Group on Indonesia (CGI). Jakarta would appoint a "Papua Coordinator" to work with national experts and international specialists participating in an "Advisory Group for Special Autonomy" and a "Papua Professional Corps" to build local capacity for effective, transparent, and accountable self-governance.

Ultimately, responsibility for conflict prevention rests with Indonesia's leaders and Papuan authorities. We hope that the Commission's involvement provides new ideas advancing shared interests and common purposes.

There are many who deserve thanks. The Commission has been ably stewarded by its chairman, Admiral Dennis C. Blair. Denny's judicious leadership and deep knowledge of Southeast Asia helped the Commission thread the needle in determining constructive recommendations in the interests of all. We greatly appreciate General John W. Vessey, whose near decade-long involvement in the CPA has been essential to its success, and the director, Bill Nash, whose on-the-ground experience and dedication has made the Center an effective instrument for preventive action. A great deal of the credit for the Commission rests with David L. Phillips, whose tireless work was indispensable. As the CPA's deputy director, David brings enthusiasm and energy to all of the CPA's endeavors. We are also most grateful to the Hewlett Foundation for its generous support.

Leslie H. Gelb
President
Council on Foreign Relations

EXECUTIVE SUMMARY

This report, *Indonesia Commission: Peace and Progress in Papua,* focuses on Papua—a remote, resource-rich, yet impoverished part of Indonesia. Unless the people of Papua are accorded greater self-governance and more benefit from the development of Papua's natural resources, continued conflict could cause a spiral of violence in Papua. It could also have a destabilizing effect elsewhere in Indonesia by encouraging ethnic, religious, and separatist violence across the vast archipelago.

Full implementation of the Special Autonomy Law would represent a win-win situation. For this to happen, the people of Papua would see that Special Autonomy is about democratization, rather than a mechanism to foreclose their concept of *merdeka*.[1] In addition, Indonesian authorities would see that Special Autonomy is about satisfying the legitimate concerns of ethnic Papuans, rather than an interim step to political independence. International stakeholders can help through a more focused and energetic approach, building local capacity to implement the Special Autonomy Law. Realizing tangible benefits for the people of Papua would also marginalize those who use violence to achieve political objectives.

The government of Indonesia has identified Papua as a priority for 2003. Improving the situation in Papua requires cooperation between the Indonesian government, Papuan authorities, and the people of Papua. Though conflict prevention is the responsibility of the parties to the conflict, the Commission also highlights the role of international stakeholders in fostering cooperation.

---

[1] *Merdeka* is an Indonesian term generally associated with secessionist political movements. It has taken on a unique significance in Papua. For most ethnic Papuans, *merdeka* refers to a utopian vision of "freedom" that is not simply political. It is a liberation theology that includes an end to repression.

BACKGROUND

Indonesia's recent progress toward a more open society provides an opportunity to deal with problems from the past. There has been controversy ever since the Netherlands ceded control of most of its former territories to the Republic of Indonesia, on December 27, 1949, while retaining Papua. Twenty years later, on August 15, 1969, Papuan delegates voted unanimously to join the Indonesian republic. However, some independent observers and many Papuans maintain that the process was flawed and illegitimate. In June 2000, 25,000 ethnic Papuans from 253 tribes elected the Papua Presidium Council (PDP) to represent their nonviolent aspirations for independence.

After the fall of President Suharto, Jakarta embarked on a course of political reform that included nationwide decentralization. In a further effort to address the demands of the people of Papua, the People's Consultative Assembly (MPR) promulgated the Special Autonomy Law for Papua (October 22, 2001). When implemented, the Special Autonomy Law will return 80 percent of royalties from mining, forestry, and fisheries, and 70 percent from oil and gas, to the province. Today, despite Papua's vast mineral, energy, and forestry resources, its people remain among the poorest in Indonesia.

Local dissatisfaction is fueled by delayed implementation of the Special Autonomy Law, harsh actions by security forces, and the frustrated aspirations of many Papuans. To make administration and social services more accessible to residents in rural areas, on January 27, 2003, President Megawati Sukarnoputri issued a Presidential Instruction dividing Papua into three provinces. Leaders in Papua have reacted critically. They view the instruction as an attempt to divide the people of Papua and to undermine reforms promised through the Special Autonomy Law. The proposed division has exacerbated tensions and increased prospects for conflict.

Indonesia has made significant progress since 1998. However, the country still faces serious challenges. To address these challenges, the Commission recommends focusing on intensified democratization, decentralization, and, in the case of Papua, implementation of the Special Autonomy Law. The Commission also calls for more discriminate and accountable security practices, greater and more widespread local benefit from the province's natural wealth, and a process for justice and reconciliation. The Commission proposes mechanisms for monitoring progress, as well as a strategy for donor and policy coordination.

Recommendations focus on the role of the United States and other international stakeholders in encouraging and enabling full implementation of the Special Autonomy Law. While there are many international stakeholders, the Commission recognizes the special history of significant cooperation between the United States and Indonesia. The United States wants to support Indonesia's efforts toward consolidating democratic reforms and enhancing national stability. It also wants to safeguard the commercial interests of American firms that have invested a total of $25 billion and, in 2001, exported $3.3 billion in goods and services to Indonesia. Security concerns have heightened for both countries since September 11, and the bombing of the nightclub in Bali has led to expanded international cooperation in the fight against terrorism.

Relations between Indonesia and the United States were in a difficult stage during the early months of 2003. As of this report's publication, the Commission's request to visit Indonesia, including Papua, had not been approved.

THE COMMISSION'S APPROACH

The *Indonesia Commission: Peace and Progress in Papua* is an initiative of the Council on Foreign Relations' Center for Preventive Action (CPA). The Commission is a results-oriented enterprise providing findings and recommendations for preventing deadly conflict. Though primary responsibility for conflict prevention rests with the government of Indonesia and leaders in Papua, the Commission recommends supporting and reinforcing actions by international stakeholders—governments, international organizations, businesses, and nongovernmental organizations (NGOs).

Effective and timely conflict prevention requires Jakarta's cooperation and leadership. Indonesia is a proud nation. It strongly resists unsolicited involvement in its internal affairs. Though the December 9, 2002, agreement between the Indonesian government and separatists from Aceh was widely seen by the international community as a positive step resolving a long-standing conflict, to some Indonesians the agreement exemplified how separatists gain strength when foreigners get involved. The same concern exists in the case of Papua. On February 5, 2003, Coordinating Minister of Political and Security Affairs Susilo Bambang Yudhoyono underscored the government's determination to prevent foreign support for separatism in Papua.

The cornerstone of the CPA's approach is the use of "carrots and sticks" by international stakeholders to encourage implementation by the government of reforms set in motion by the Special Autonomy Law. The Commission recognizes the Indonesian government's concerns. It emphasizes the positive inducement of foreign aid as the most effective incentive available to international stakeholders. To use scarce development resources most wisely, the Commission believes that development assistance can be sharpened by linking conflict prevention goals with socioeconomic development programs ("preventive development"). This would enable stakeholders to better coordinate and work more effectively with Indonesian government and Papuan officials. The report highlights existing organizations and mechanisms for official development assistance (ODA).

FINDINGS AND RECOMMENDATIONS

With the goal of enhancing the benefits of Special Autonomy, the Commission focuses on (a) governance, (b) the economy, (c) security, (d) social development, and (e) justice and reconciliation. Recommendations in each category are intended to maximize benefits to Indonesia and to the people of Papua from democratization, decentralization, and economic development. Recommendations also seek to create a context for effective and full implementation of the Special Autonomy Law.

[4]

Governance

Governance under President Suharto was characterized by virtual single-party rule, a strong nationwide security presence, and centralization of power and wealth. Basic social services, especially in Papua's rural areas, improved but did not keep pace with improvements elsewhere in Indonesia. Many Papuans continued to rely for their basic needs on local systems of organization associated with churches and based on *adat* (traditional modes of tribal and clan politics).

In 1999, President B. J. Habibie initiated a national decentralization plan to devolve a greater share of authority and revenue to local governments. As a further step toward more local control of Papua's natural resources, Special Autonomy for Papua *(Otonomi Khusus)* was adopted during the administration of Habibie's successor, President Abdurrahman Wahid. This law went even further in providing for Papua to retain up to 80 percent of the income derived from the province's extractive industries.

The task of implementing Special Autonomy has been hindered by competing priorities in Jakarta, a heritage of mutual distrust, and, due to a lack of training and experience, inadequate capacity in Papua to handle increased responsibilities. The Presidential Instruction dividing Papua into three provinces was issued without consent from the Papua People's Assembly (MRP). This body, provided for in the Special Autonomy Law, has not yet been formed.

The Commission believes effective implementation of the Special Autonomy Law is central to reducing tensions in Papua. To address Jakarta's concerns about stability and promote greater self-government for Papua through implementation of the Special Autonomy Law, the Commission recommends that

- The Indonesian government postpone any plan to divide Papua into three provinces and instead accelerate full implementation of the Special Autonomy Law. Any further action on the province's reorganization would be taken in consultation with the MRP, to be formed expeditiously.

- The Indonesian government appoint a widely respected and experienced Indonesian as "Papua Coordinator." Assisted by national experts and international specialists as part of a "Special Autonomy Advisory Group," the Papua Coordinator would work with provincial authorities to draft laws and regulations required for implementing Special Autonomy.
- The United Nations Development Programme (UNDP), in coordination with the World Bank's Consultative Group on Indonesia (CGI), establish a "Papua Professional Corps" of national experts and international specialists sponsored by donor countries, international businesses, and NGOs to assist with social and economic development projects and to participate in the Special Autonomy Advisory Group.
- The CGI work with the Indonesian government and Papuan provincial officials to assess and improve local capacity for improved governance, including management, budgeting, and administration.
- The U.S. Agency for International Development (USAID) and other donors support a public education program focusing on "democratization," aimed at generating understanding and support for Special Autonomy.

The Economy

Despite progress since the financial crisis of 1997–98, Indonesia's national economy is still affected by high external debt and non-performing domestic loans. The Bali bombing, which may cost more than $1 billion in lost revenues, has further discouraged foreign direct investment (FDI). Burdensome regulations at the national and provincial levels also discourage FDI. To address the budget deficit and repay debt, the CGI recently agreed to a new $2.7 billion loan (January 20, 2003). The International Monetary Fund (IMF) is encouraging legal measures that mitigate corruption, as well as protections against political influence in business in order to stimulate investments, including FDI.

Papua's resource extraction consistently generates profits and tax revenues. In Papua, Freeport-McMoRan Copper & Gold Inc. (henceforth in this report referred to as Freeport) operates the world's largest gold and copper mine. It is the single largest tax-payer in Indonesia and the largest employer in Papua. Ethnic Papuans currently make up 26 percent of Freeport employees in Papua. Logging in Papua generates about $100 million annually to the central government. Since 1997, BP (formerly British Petroleum) and BPMIGAS (Badan Pelaksana Migas), the government petroleum-resource regulator, have been developing the Tangguh natural-gas field. When that field comes on line in 2007, Tangguh liquefied natural gas (LNG) will be exported to China's Fujian Province.

Papua has vast natural resources. However, they are not fully developed and the economic activity they generate has not contributed considerably to economic development benefiting ethnic Papuans. Despite overall improvement in social services since the 1960s, most ethnic Papuans are still engaged in subsistence activities, including hunting, fishing, and agriculture. Papua's urban economy is almost entirely in the hands of non-ethnic Papuan migrants. The 2001 UNDP Human Development Index ranked Papua as Indonesia's second poorest province, behind West Nusa Tenggara.

The Commission believes that economic development resulting in more and better-paying jobs in Papua will both improve livelihoods and moderate dissatisfaction. The Commission recommends that

- The national and provincial authorities, including the governor and the Provincial People's Legislative Council (DPRD), prepare a province-wide master plan for sustainable resource development. Necessary expertise may be sought from stakeholder governments, international businesses, and NGOs.
- The Indonesian government make foreign investment regulations more competitive at the national and provincial levels, particularly with respect to the resource industries of mining, forestry, and petroleum.
- National and provincial authorities apply funds made available to the province from revenue-sharing required by decentralization to support business training, microcredit, rural cooperatives, quick impact, and employment-generation projects for ethnic Papuans.

- National and provincial authorities sustain a campaign against corruption, including the setup of an Anticorruption Commission in Papua, and donors support the Papua Chamber of Commerce in conducting ethics and anticorruption training.
- National and provincial authorities, in consultation with the CGI, establish a "Papua Professional Corps" to assist donor-sponsored social and economic development projects and work in provincial government departments.
- International businesses, working with the Indonesian government and the Special Autonomy Advisory Group, initiate procedures for greater transparency of revenue transfers between businesses and central, provincial, and district governments per the "Publish What You Pay" NGO initiative, which requires businesses to fully disclose tax and royalty payments.
- International and national businesses sustain and enhance training and hiring of ethnic Papuans.

Security

The Indonesian National Army (TNI) and the Indonesian National Police (POLRI) have a strong presence in Papua and other provinces where there is violence or an independence movement. TNI receives only 25–30 percent of its budget from the national government. It raises the rest through legal and illegal activities. Though there is no external threat to Papua, Indonesian law requires TNI security for "national assets." TNI therefore provides security for mining and energy operations in Papua. Security payments to TNI by international companies contribute to corruption among underpaid and undisciplined TNI personnel.

National-level reforms to improve the training and tighten the central control of TNI have not taken full effect at the local level. In regions such as Papua, Jakarta has not been able to assert complete control over local security activities. Training of officers and troops is uneven, and troops are not held accountable for killing or injuring Papuans, or for damaging property.

There have been some developments. On April 21, 2003, seven soldiers of TNI Special Forces (KOPASSUS) were convicted of killing Papua Presidium Council (PDP) Chairman Theys Eluay and sentenced to prison terms of up to 42 months. TNI and POLRI are cooperating with the U.S. Federal Bureau of Investigation (FBI) to investigate the killing in Tembagapura of two Americans and one Indonesian working for Freeport (August 31, 2002). TNI has also announced plans to crack down on illegal logging in Papua.

The Commission believes that a better-trained, adequately paid, and more accountable security force in Papua is essential to provide law, order, and security while decreasing resentments, which fuel pro-independence sentiment. The Commission recommends that

- The Indonesian government and TNI place tight limits on the activities of TNI Special Forces (KOPASSUS) and over time remove KOPASSUS from Papua.
- POLRI continue its responsibility for law and order. In this context, POLRI would reformulate the mandate and mission of its Mobile Brigade (BRIMOB) in Papua to strictly conform with regular police activities.
- Donor military and police assistance programs develop plans, in conjunction with TNI and the Provincial Police (POLDA), concentrating advisory and training activities on units in Papua and focusing on effective security procedures that respect the rights of citizens and emphasize community-based policing.
- TNI and POLDA follow up recent successes cracking down on illegal logging by further reducing the involvement of their personnel in illicit activities.
- The Indonesian government revise the law on the protection of national assets to end the requirement that businesses use TNI for security contracts, so that private local security organizations can be developed.
- International businesses operating in Papua gradually phase out their security service contracts with TNI, as changes in Indonesian law permit, and report on their compliance with the "Voluntary Principles on Security and Human Rights."

Social Development

Changing demographics and patterns of economic development are eroding traditional values and institutions in the province. Papua's population of 2.1 million includes approximately 800,000 migrants from other parts of Indonesia who dominate the civil service and control local business. Social services for many ethnic Papuans are provided by traditional *adat* institutions and informal organizations associated with the Protestant and Catholic churches. Most ethnic Papuans receive little schooling, and Papua's health sector suffers from neglect and inadequate budgetary support.

The Commission believes that substantial improvement in social services will help meet the basic needs of Papuans and that the delivery of improved services will build confidence in the public sector. The Commission recommends that

- The national government and authorities in Papua apply funds from donors to strengthen education and health programs in Papua, including training, to bring standards in line with conditions elsewhere in Indonesia.
- Stakeholder government-aid organizations active in Indonesia expand and coordinate their programs in Papua, with emphasis on serving populations in remote areas.

Justice and Reconciliation

President Megawati apologized for past policy mistakes and army excesses in Papua during Independence Day celebrations in 2001. There is still much to be done, however, in strengthening the rule of law, bringing human rights offenders to justice, protecting local human rights workers, and overcoming the legacy of injustice. Some independent observers and many Papuans see the 1969 Act of Free Choice, by which Papua acceded to Jakarta's authority, as flawed and illegitimate. Pro-independence activists are seeking "historical rectification" and *merdeka.*

The Commission believes there must be accountability and a process for acknowledging Papua's violent history and promoting improved intergroup relations. The Commission recommends that

- The national government and authorities in Papua ensure that persons responsible for human rights abuses are prosecuted before impartial courts staffed by independent judges and prosecutors.

- The Indonesian government, in consultation with leaders in Papua such as the governor, Provincial People's Legislative Council members, and civil society and religious leaders, designate a "Reconciliation Group," led by a prominent individual, to consult with the people of Papua, national experts, and international specialists on reenergizing the "National Dialogue" and developing an appropriate truth, justice, and reconciliation process for Papua as called for in the Special Autonomy Law.

- Donors, international organizations, and businesses operating in Papua provide additional support to local organizations involved in human rights education and monitoring.

- Religious, ethnic-based, and tribal organizations continue their dialogue on the peaceful resolution of disputes, and donor resources be used to institutionalize the dialogue through the strengthening of a permanent governing body (e.g., the Papua Peace Commission).

Policy Coordination

Papua receives most international attention when there is an incident of violence, such as the murder of a foreigner or a prominent Papuan, or at international meetings when the question of Papuan independence is raised. Under these circumstances, Indonesia is continually on the defensive. The Commission encourages the Indonesian government to take steps to engage stakeholders in a positive way by, for example, securing their support for implementation of the Special Autonomy Law. The Commission further recommends that

- The Indonesian government assign the "Papua Coordinator" responsibility for raising the profile of Papuan issues in Jakarta, enhancing interagency communications, fostering an ongoing dialogue between Indonesian officials and leaders in Papua, and constructively involving international stake-holders.

- Donors support a "Papua Monitoring Group" composed of experts in Jakarta and Papua to monitor conditions, inform policy decisions, and raise international awareness about urgent problems in Papua.
- Stakeholder governments increase the attention paid to Papua through more frequent visits by ambassadors and other officials, and by including Papua on the agenda of bilateral and multilateral discussions.

Stakeholder Coordination

To enhance donor coordination and use scarce development resources more wisely, the Commission recommends that

- The European Commission (EC) propose and secure support for adoption of a "Preventive Development Program" at the next meeting of the CGI.
- The UNDP and donor countries conduct a "Preventive Development Assessment" to review existing conflict-prevention activities, identify programming gaps, and develop an overall preventive development strategy for Papua.
- The CGI draw on its members to establish a "Papua Committee" with donor affinity groups (DAGs) to assist with donor coordination and raise new funds for activities developed as part of the Preventive Development Program.
- A donor, such as Japan, host a conference to launch the Preventive Development Program.

The European Union (EU) is best suited to propose the Preventive Development Program as a follow-up to its "2001 Conflict Prevention Assessment Mission to Indonesia," which was welcomed by the Indonesian government.

The World Bank Consultative Group on Indonesia coordinates financing among its thirty members (multilateral agencies and donor countries). To help Indonesia recover from the Asian financial crisis (1997–98), the World Bank provided $4.5 billion as part of an IMF-led assistance program in place since 1997. At a recent

World Bank conference (January 20, 2003), donors agreed to a new $2.7 billion package.

The United Nations Development Programme works with specialized United Nations (UN) agencies linking social and economic development with conflict prevention. In addition, the UNDP's Partnership for Governance Reform supports decentralization and Special Autonomy. The UN has made considerable progress restoring friendly and constructive relations with the Indonesian government, which initially resented the UN's stewardship of East Timor's independence.

Japan is proposed as the convener of a donor conference to launch the Preventive Development Program. In the Asia-Pacific region, Japan has a proven interest in "development for peace." As the largest donor to Indonesia, Japan's contributions averaged $1.9 billion a year in the 1990s.

Donor affinity groups would bring together donor countries and organizations to further coordinate assistance and focus aid on conflict prevention. The U.S. Agency for International Development has integrated conflict prevention into its overall country strategy through its Indonesia Office of Conflict Prevention and Response (OCPR). The Netherlands has a special interest in Papua due to its historical ties to the province. The Dutch Ministry for International Cooperation and Development and the Canadian International Development Agency (CIDA) support governance with special emphasis on decentralization. Since the Bali bombing, Australia has taken steps to strengthen its cooperation with Indonesia. The Australian Agency for International Development (AusAID) focuses on Indonesia's eastern islands, including Papua. Other donors, such as the United Kingdom's Department for International Development (DFID) and Germany's Bank for Reconstruction and Development (KfW), support the UNDP's Bureau for Crisis Prevention and Recovery (BCPR).

Neighboring countries and regional associations can play the most useful role moderating extremism among the people of Papua. Papua New Guinea (PNG) knows the danger of militant self-determination movements, having waged its own ten-year war with the Bougainville Revolutionary Army. Newly independent

East Timor supports decentralization for securing the political and cultural rights of the people of Papua. Vanuatu, Nauru, and the Solomon Islands are in close contact with leaders in Papua and could act as a moderating influence. The Pacific Islands Forum (formerly South Pacific Forum), which adopted a resolution in August 2002 stating that Papua is an integral part of Indonesia, could also act as such.

International businesses can further promote moderation by promoting project benefits with the people of Papua. Such activities are already underway and should be expanded. Freeport established the Voluntary Land Rights Trust Fund in 2001. Its One Percent Fund provides up to $18 million annually for education, health, business, and infrastructure in Papua. BP is collaborating with USAID and local government representatives to implement a diversified growth strategy channeling investments to towns; BP is also developing innovative community-based security arrangements.

International NGOs can also play a role. Transparency International, which provides technical assistance to anticorruption efforts, is active in Indonesia. The "Publish What You Pay" initiative of the Open Society Institute (OSI) encourages major multinational corporations to disclose their balance sheets. InterNews supports several radio stations and newspapers in Papua, and produces "Reporting for Peace" radio programs.

The *Indonesia Commission: Peace and Progress in Papua* proposes to host a meeting of Indonesian officials and Papuan leaders for the purpose of discussing its findings and recommendations. It believes that this report can serve as a starting point for promoting trust, building confidence, and enhancing conflict prevention. The Commission will not, however, act as a mediator.

INDONESIA

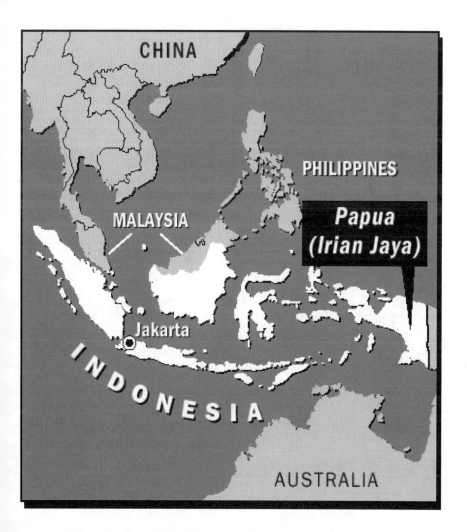

PROPOSED INITIATIVES AND STRUCTURES

Structure	Implementing Agency	Function
Policy Coordination		
Papua Coordinator	Indonesian government	Raise the profile of Papuan issues in Jakarta
		Enhance interagency communications
		Foster dialogue between Indonesian officials and leaders in Papua, and involve international stakeholders
		Work with the Special Autonomy Advisory Group to draft laws and regulations required for implementation of Special Autonomy
Papua Monitoring Group	Center for Strategic and International Studies, Jakarta	Monitor and report on progress and problems affecting conflict conditions
Stakeholder Coordination		
Papua Committee/Donor Affinity Groups	CGI	Assist with donor coordination and raise new funds
Governance		
Special Autonomy Advisory Group	Indonesian government/ authorities in Papua	Help draft laws and regulations required for implementing Special Autonomy

Papua Professional Corps	UNDP/CGI	Assist with donor-sponsored social and economic development projects Work in provincial government departments Participate in Special Autonomy Advisory Group
Oversight Bureau	DPRD	Ensure fair and equal participation for ethnic Papuans in the civil service

The Economy

Anticorruption Commission	Indonesian government/ DPRD	Raise awareness and counter corruption Conduct anticorruption training

Justice and Reconciliation

Reconciliation Group	Indonesian government/ leaders in Papua	Consult with national experts and international specialists on a truth, justice, and reconciliation process for Papua
Papua Branch of the TNI Inspector General	TNI	Raise awareness and counter corruption
Papua Branch of the POLRI Office of Professional Responsibility	POLRI/POLDA	Raise awareness and counter corruption

REPORT

INTRODUCTION

The *Indonesia Commission: Peace and Progress in Papua* is an initiative of the Council on Foreign Relations' Center for Preventive Action (CPA). The Commission is a results-oriented enterprise focused on producing findings and recommendations for preventing a spiral of deadly conflict in Papua. It recommends how national and local leaders, with the support of international stakeholders, can advance the goal of conflict prevention.

WHY INDONESIA?

By virtue of its size, location, and population, Indonesia is widely recognized as the most strategically important country in Southeast Asia. Since the Asian financial crisis of the late 1990s and the fall of President Suharto in 1998, Indonesia has made positive if uneven progress toward economic recovery and democratic governance. Indonesia's success is important for the region and the world.

Indonesia has an important role to play in the global campaign against terrorism. It has the world's largest Muslim population, with over 200 million practitioners, including a small minority who support fundamentalist Muslim objectives. Its large size and overstretched security forces make Indonesia a potential base for terrorist organizations. Following the August 2002 bombing of a nightclub in Bali, it has moved aggressively and successfully to pursue Jemaah Islamiyah, the Islamic militant group responsible for the bombing.

There are important economic reasons for conflict prevention in Indonesia. U.S.-based multinational corporations (MNCs) have invested $25 billion in Indonesia. In 2001, U.S. firms exported $3.3 billion in goods and services to Indonesia. The U.S. Export-Import Bank, the Overseas Private Investment Corporation, and the Trade Development Agency provided $400 million in credits to finance U.S. exports to Indonesia in 2002.[2] The Malacca Strait, off the coast of northern Sumatra, is the world's second busiest international shipping route.

WHY PAPUA?

Indonesia's largest and easternmost province, Papua, has long been considered important for its resource wealth, cultural heritage, and biological diversity. Papua also hosts some of the country's largest current and projected investment projects by foreign corporations—in particular, the mining operations of Freeport and a planned natural-gas field at Tangguh to be operated by BP.

Papua is also one of Indonesia's most troubled regions. Indonesia is now at a crossroads in Papua. A cycle of violence lies down one path. Repressive measures would fuel resentment, increase opposition to the government, and intensify demands for political independence. An escalation of the conflict could heighten international concerns and calls for humanitarian intervention, while dissuading foreign investors. In the worst case, troubles in Papua could adversely affect the national stability of Indonesia.

Down the other path lies mutual accommodation and reconciliation realized through dialogue. This course requires the people of Papua to accept the benefits to be derived from a fully implemented Special Autonomy Law, and for the governance of Indonesia to allow the people of Papua greater self-governance and a greater financial return from development of the province's natural resources. Mutual accommodation is in the interests of the people of Papua, the national government, and the international community, including the United States.

The Commission is also concerned about armed conflict displacing civilians and causing human hardship. Deadly violence in Papua could send populations across borders to Papua New

---

[2] In 2001, U.S. direct investments in Indonesia accounted for $8.807 billion (on a historical-cost basis). U.S. Department of Commerce, Bureau of Economic Analysis, www.bea.doc.gov/bea/di/dia-ctry.htm.

Guinea (PNG) and across the sea to Australia. It could spread to other conflict-prone areas in Indonesia, thereby triggering widespread violence and endangering national unity. In contrast, progress in Papua would establish momentum toward enhanced conflict prevention nationwide.

Prominent Indonesians have urged that the Commission focus its efforts there. In addition, Papuan political, church, and civil society leaders have indicated that the CPA can play an important role generating new ideas and energizing the Indonesian government and leaders in Papua. The Commission believes the time is right for concerted action on Papua and that its involvement can add value and make a difference. While the Commission was conducting this study, the Indonesian government identified Papua as a priority for 2003.

CONDITIONS IN PAPUA

Located in the far eastern end of the vast Indonesian archipelago, Papua has an estimated population of 2.1 million people[3], including approximately 800,000 migrants.[4] Its vast territory of 421,918 square kilometers has the lowest population density in Indonesia. Ethnically Melanesian (unlike the ethnic Malays who make up the vast majority of Indonesia's population), Papua's diverse peoples comprise hundreds of tribal groups and 250 distinct languages. Most ethnic Papuans live in remote rural settings where they practice Christianity and animism. Until a few decades ago, many tribes living in the rugged interior of the province had little or no contact with the outside world. The Dani tribe, with a

---

[3] BPS Statistics Indonesia, "Indonesia's 2000 Population Census," Bangkok, 29 November 2000. The total population of Papua was estimated at 2,112,756. Because of the "unstable situation" in Papua, the enumeration was carried out "only in areas with condusive situations for census undertakng."

[4] Information provided by the UNDP in Jakarta.

population of nearly 400,000, was discovered only when a plane first flew over the Baliem Valley in 1938.

In recent decades, internal migration has changed Papua's ethnic composition. Beginning in the 1980s, Indonesia's Transmigration Program resettled inhabitants of densely populated regions of Indonesia to Papua. To accommodate these new arrivals, authorities often relocated indigenous communities from their traditional lands. Spontaneous migration also surged during the 1990s. Today migrants from western Indonesia dominate both the civil service and the local economy in Papua.[5] These changing demographics have dramatically increased wealth disparities and social tension in the region.

Since 1969, Papua has benefited from the overall improvements in security and prosperity of Indonesia. Overall living conditions in the province in absolute terms are unquestionably better than they were 40 years ago. Indonesia itself is not a well-off country. Measuring country performance in terms of life expectancy, adjusted real income, and education levels, the 2002 United Nations Development Programme (UNDP) Human Development Index ranks Indonesia 110th out of 173 countries. In relative terms, however, Papua has not kept pace with economic progress in the rest of Indonesia. Within Indonesia, Papua is the second poorest province, after West Nusa Tenggara.[6]

Papua's natural wealth lies in its forests, mineral deposits, and hydrocarbon fields. Experts estimate that most of Papua's natural resources have yet to be tapped. Biologically resplendent rainforests account for approximately 34.6 million hectares, or 24 percent of Indonesia's total forested area, and 54 percent of Indonesia's biodiversity.[7]

---

[5] "Indonesia: Ending Repression in Irian Jaya."

[6] United Nations Development Programme (UNDP), *Human Development Report 2002: Deepening Democracy in a Fragmented World*, 24 July 2002, available at hdr.undp.org. See also UNDP, *Making New Technologies Work for Human Development: Human Development Report 2001* (New York: Oxford University Press, 2001).

[7] Australia West Papua Association, "West Papua Information Kit" (Department of Computer Sciences, University of Texas at Austin). See also the Biodiversity Conservation Project in Indonesia, the World Resources Institute's Sustainable Development Information Services, and http://www.geocities.com/RainForest/4466/biodiver.htm.

The largest current resource-extraction enterprise in Papua is Freeport's gold and copper mine, the world's largest. Like many mining operations around the world, this operation has been both a benefit and a source of controversy in Papua. Natural-gas fields are operated by several companies, with a large operation being developed in Tangguh by BP. Timber is harvested by many different Indonesian and foreign companies, with illegal logging on the increase, despite recent efforts by the Indonesian government to enforce regulations.

POLITICAL HISTORY

On December 27, 1949, following a prolonged struggle, the Netherlands ceded independence to its former territories, except West New Guinea (then named Irian Jaya and now called Papua). The agreement specified that "the question of the political status of New Guinea be determined through negotiations" between the Netherlands and Indonesia within a year of the transfer of sovereignty.

Papua's legal status remained in limbo until the United States placed heavy pressure on the Dutch and brokered an agreement transferring administrative authority for West New Guinea from the Netherlands to the United Nations (UN). Article 18 of the 1962 New York Agreement specified that "Indonesia will make arrangements with the assistance and participation of the United Nations" for giving Papuans the opportunity to choose whether or not to become a part of Indonesia.[8] Selected delegates voted unanimously on August 15, 1969, to join the republic. The Act of Free Choice was accepted by the UN General Assembly, and West New Guinea, renamed Irian Jaya, became the 27th province of Indonesia on November 19, 1969. Pro-independence advocates question this process.

---

[8] The New York Agreement, Article 18 (New York: United Nations, 15 August 1962).

These events occurred against the backdrop of tumult elsewhere in Indonesia. Political violence resulted in the deaths of at least 500,000 persons.[9] The victorious General Suharto imposed a "New Order" with strict controls to ensure stability and development. At the same time, the regime's heavily centralized approach to governance, "*pancasila*[10] democracy," generated resentment in Papua.

In accordance with its Dual Function *(dwi fungsi)* mandate, the Indonesian National Army (TNI) broadened its presence to secure the country's territorial integrity and protect investments in Papua's emerging minerals industry. In addition, the armed forces were charged with providing security to western Indonesian migrants resettled in Papua under the national government's transmigration program. Relocation programs, land seizures, and control of the economy by the newly arrived transmigrants increasingly displaced ethnic Papuans and reduced their power in the political process. Today non-ethnic Papuans represent about 40 percent of Papua's total population while dominating both the local economy and the province's civil service.[11] The Free Papua Movement (OPM), which emerged as a militant pro-independence group in the 1960s, continues as a local, low-grade but persistent secessionist struggle.

RECENT DEVELOPMENTS

The Asian financial crisis (1997–98) precipitated a series of events, including public protests, that resulted in the downfall of President Suharto's regime in May 1998. After a brief transition period stewarded by Vice President B. J. Habibie, Indonesia conducted its first free election in four decades. Although the party of Megawati Sukarnoputri, the daughter of Sukarno, Indonesia's

---

[9] Robert Cribb, ed., *The Indonesian Killings 1965–1966: Studies from Java and Bali* (Monash University, Southeast Asia Publications, January 1991).

[10] The state philosophy based on five interrelated principles: belief in one supreme God; just and civilized humanitarianism; nationalism as expressed in the unity of Indonesia; popular sovereignty arrived at through deliberation and democracy; and social justice for all the Indonesian people.

[11] "Indonesia: Ending Repression in Irian Jaya."

founding leader, received the most votes, the national parliament chose a moderate Islamic leader, Abdurrahman Wahid, as president in July 1999; President Wahid selected Mrs. Megawati as vice president. During the interim period before Wahid's assumed office, an Indonesian-proposed and UN-supervised referendum in East Timor resulted in a vote for independence, followed by a period of violence that led to the deployment of a UN peacekeeping force to East Timor. Mrs. Megawati succeeded President Wahid when he was pushed aside after 20 months in office. President Megawati is only the second president of Indonesia to achieve the nation's highest office via a peaceful transfer of power. She has fostered consensus and cooperation through a diverse cabinet.

The August 2002 constitutional amendment provides for Indonesians to directly elect the executive for the first time when they go to the polls in 2004. The president and vice president have until recently been chosen by the People's Consultative Assembly (MPR), which includes 500 representatives from the elected parliament and 200 non-elected representatives. A Regional Representative Council (DPD) has been established to give provincial representatives a stronger voice at the national level.

The parliament is also playing a key role in preserving Indonesia's secular administration. The MPR pushed back a renewed effort by Islamic groups and Vice President Hamzah Haz to adopt shari'a, or Islamic law. Although the two largest Muslim organizations in the country, the Nahdlatul Ulama and the Muhammadiyah, are moderate and support the secular state, there is broad and growing popular support for more radical Islamist groups. Laskar Jihad has been formally disbanded, but is still active.

Political and administrative actions have also been taken in Papua during this very unsettled period. As an indication of the resentment or apathy most Papuans felt toward the Indonesian political process, well more than half of ethnic Papuans boycotted the national elections in 1999.[12] In an effort to address the acute social

---

[12] These estimates were supplied by Indonesian Election Watch (IEW), an ad hoc body of national and international academics and nongovernmental organizations organized for the 1999 elections. IEW conducted significant research in Papua during the 1999 general elections.

and political problems in Papua, and to provide greater self-governance and more local ownership of natural resources, the Indonesian central government proposed the Special Autonomy Law for Papua. Passed by the People's Legislative Council (DPR) in October 2001, the Special Autonomy Law requires redistribution of 80 percent of local forestry, fishery, and mining revenues and 70 percent of oil and gas income back to provincial and district authorities. Special Autonomy reaffirms traditional "customary law" and creates institutions to voice Papuan aspirations and promote indigenous rights. It also liberalizes the formation of political parties, creates village consultative bodies, and provides for the resolution of land conflicts via *adat* mediation mechanisms. Regulations allow Irian Jaya to be called Papua and relax restrictions on the flying of the Papuan "Morning Star" flag.

In an unprecedented display of unity, 25,000 ethnic Papuans representing 253 tribes elected, on June 5, 2000, the Papua Presidium Council (PDP) to represent their nonviolent democratic aspirations. Despite the murder of its chairman, Theys Eluay, on November 11, 2001, the PDP remains the leading voice of ethnic Papuans. So far, however, implementation of decentralization and the Special Autonomy Law has been slow, and this has exacerbated the frustrations of most Papuans. Papuan political leaders are intensifying their demands for "historical rectification" as an effort to set the record straight on Papua's incorporation into Indonesia, and to assert Papuan identity. Papuan appeals for *merdeka* are persistent and powerful.

THE MEANINGS OF *MERDEKA* AND *OTONOMI*

Words matter, and it is important to understand two terms that play defining roles in the political discourse in Papua. The word *merdeka* is often translated as "political independence," and this meaning poses a fundamental challenge to Indonesians concerned about their country's territorial integrity. For ethnic Papuans, the term might be better translated as "freedom"—in particular, freedom from oppression, discrimination, and injustice. Currently, *merdeka* sentiments cut across class as well as regional and tribal affiliations among ethnic Papuans.

Otonomi, or autonomy, is the term for the concept embodied in the Special Autonomy Law. To Indonesian authorities the important aspect of *otonomi* is that it preserves the territorial integrity of their country, while granting unique, limited self-governance and resources to the province.

Today's political discourse is deadlocked between these two seemingly irreconcilable conceptions: *merdeka* and *otonomi.* For many ethnic Papuans the future is seen as a mutually exclusive choice between the two. To break this deadlock, *merdeka* must be better understood as a suprapolitical concept—both more and less than a struggle for political independence—and the concept of *otonomi* must be understood to provide the improved living standards, self-governing authority, and personal freedoms that are compatible with the wider meaning of *merdeka.*

Meaning justice, equality, and democracy, *merdeka* is a state of being, not necessarily an end state.[13] In this light, it may be possible to achieve *merdeka* without realizing political statehood. This can be achieved only if there is real progress in Papua. As a traditional form of conflict prevention, *merdeka* could represent the key to resolving differences between the people of Papua and the government of Indonesia.

---

[13] Brigham M. Golden, "Letter to the Editor," *The Van Zorge Report on Indonesia,* Vol. II, No. 20 (Jakarta, 30 November 2000).

INTERNATIONAL STAKEHOLDERS

The prevention strategy of the Center for Preventive Action (CPA) seeks to not only involve key national and local actors in finding peaceful solutions to conflicts, but also to mobilize international stakeholders. Such stakeholders have the potential to influence the process toward peace and progress. Recommendations in this report target those with direct responsibility in Papua. They also highlight supporting actions by stakeholders. This chapter summarizes the many countries, international organizations, and businesses that are already involved in Indonesia and Papua.

KEY COUNTRIES

The United States is committed to consolidating Indonesia's political and economic reform, and to working with Indonesia to counter terrorism. The United States can influence political and economic reform, as well as reform of the security sector. Military-to-military contact may give the United States improved channels to encourage security-sector reform, enable more effective cooperation in combating terrorism, and help encourage human rights. In 2001, the U.S. Agency for International Development (USAID) budget was $156 million for projects in Indonesia,[14] with a special focus on eight provinces, including Papua. USAID has integrated conflict prevention into its overall country strategy via the newly established Office of Conflict Prevention and Response (OCPR). Other conflict-prevention efforts are undertaken by USAID's Office of Democracy and Governance. The Office of Foreign Disaster Assistance (OFDA) and its Food for Peace

---

[14] In 2002, USAID's Indonesia budget was $129.3 million. Its request for 2003 is $141.7 million. See www.usaid.gov.

program identify interventions that both meet food security needs and strengthen local capacities for peace-building. USAID's Performance-Oriented Management Program (PERFORM) is noteworthy for its successful efforts in building the local capacity of district-level administrators. The Civil Society Strengthening Program (CSSP) has also achieved positive results by improving the institutional and technical capacities of civil-society organizations around Indonesia, and specifically in Papua.

Several countries have programs supporting good governance. In 2002, the Dutch Ministry for International Cooperation and Development contributed $75 million bilaterally to Indonesia[15] and about $60 million to United Nations (UN) agencies. Given its history in the Dutch East Indies, the Netherlands is careful not to undertake activities that might be construed as support for separatism. The Canadian International Development Agency (CIDA) spends $43 million a year, with a priority on equity and governance.[16] Valued at $30.5 million in 2001, Germany's foreign aid assists economic and political reform, including decentralization. The German Agency for Technical Cooperation (GTZ) and the German Bank for Reconstruction and Development (KfW) are active in the field of governance, with a special interest in capacity-building for decentralization.

The Australian Agency for International Development (AusAID) expended $77.7 million in 2000, mostly on projects in eastern Indonesia.[17] After the Bali bombing, Australia has revitalized its efforts to work with Indonesia in implementing a bilateral antiterrorism agreement and eradicating conditions conducive to terrorism. Canberra also focuses its foreign aid on mitigating conflicts,

---

[15] The Netherlands Ministry of Foreign Affairs spends over $75 million annually on bilateral aid to Indonesia. In 2002, the Netherlands doubled its funding to the UN Environment Programme, and it promotes scholarly exchange between Indonesia and the Netherlands. In Indonesia, the majority of the bilateral aid from the Netherlands goes to covering basic education. Netherlands Ministry of Foreign Affairs, www.minbuza.nl; and the Embassy of the Netherlands to Indonesia, www.netherlandsembassy.or.id.

[16] The Canadian government spends about $18 million a year on bilateral aid to Indonesia. Embassy of Canada to Indonesia, www.dfait-maeci.gc.ca/jakarta/.

[17] Embassy of Australia to Indonesia, www.austembjak.or.id/.

which might precipitate population displacement. Australia is geographically close to Papua and would be the most affected by refugee flows, which could inflame domestic concerns over immigration and asylum policies. Australia's influence has, however, diminished as a result of its prominent role in UN activities in East Timor.

Other countries have a special interest in poverty reduction. The United Kingdom's Department for International Development (DFID) works with the Asian Development Bank (ADB). Germany's KfW and the Swedish International Development Agency (SIDA) also support social development activities. Norway provides humanitarian assistance through the Norwegian Red Cross. New Zealand has historical affinities with Melanesian movements and, as a leader of the Pacific Islands/Indigenous People solidarity movement, has traditionally championed human rights causes in the Pacific Islands region. Though Wellington's Labor-led coalition government includes supporters of Papua's political independence, its official policy emphasizes full and timely implementation of Special Autonomy.

Some countries highlight activities designed to advance mediation and nonviolent conflict prevention. Germany's KfW supports the Bureau for Conflict Prevention and Recovery (BCPR) of the United Nations Development Programme (UNDP). Through organizations such as the Peace Research Institute of Oslo (PRIO), Norway assists mediation and dialogue with the goal of conflict prevention around the world. Other countries whose agencies are involved in truth and reconciliation processes include New Zealand and Canada (i.e., NZAID and CIDA).

Japan has significant self-interest in Indonesia's economic reform. The Japan Bank for International Cooperation (JBIC) is the largest bilateral donor to Indonesia. Contributions from the Japan Export-Import Bank (JEXIM) and the Japanese Overseas Economic Cooperation Fund (OECF) averaged $1.9 billion a year in the mid 1990s. Japan also has extensive commercial interests in Indonesia. JAPEX (Japan Petroleum Exploration Co., Ltd.) and INPEX (INPEX Corporation, formerly Indonesia Petroleum, Ltd.) are involved in Papua's energy sector, and Japanese banks own more than $30 billion of Indonesia's external debt. While Japan would be prepared to play a leading role on macroeconomic reform, only the Japan International Cooperation Agency (JICA) supports democratization projects.[18]

In addition to Japan, other countries with significant economic interests in Indonesia have not focused on conflict prevention. For example, China wants Indonesia to exploit Papua's energy sector. It chose Tangguh to supply liquified natural gas (LNG) to Fujian Province, with supplies projected to commence in 2007. China has expressed concern about separatist violence in Papua.

Though the government of South Korea has not been active in Indonesian policy, South Korea's transition from military dictatorship to democracy makes it a useful Asian partner as Indonesia consolidates its own democratization. South Korea's Petroleum Development Corporation has a small stake in Papua's energy sector. Korean concerns are extensively involved in logging along the border with Papua New Guinea (PNG).

Singapore has granted loans and, to expand economic opportunities for Indonesia, included some Indonesian-manufactured products in its free-trade agreement with the United States. Many Singaporean investors have a considerable stake in Indonesian enterprises. For example, in December 2002, Singapore Technologies Telemedia bought a 42 percent stake in the overseas call operator Indonesia Satellite for $631 million. Through a variety of financing arrangements, Singapore could assist in enhancing Indonesia's economic development.

Papua New Guinea and Papua are adjacent territories with a similar natural environment and populations of Melanesian ethnicity. There are already approximately 7,500 Papuan refugees in PNG. In the event of conflict escalation in Papua, it is

---

[18] Japan is the largest donor to Indonesia. Japan's International Cooperation Agency and Trade and Economic Cooperation Bureau (METI) focus on loan aid rescheduling; infrastructure projects; poverty reduction through economic growth and education (including distance learning and access to information); donor (and NGO) and policy coordination, including the promotion of South-South cooperation; and human security, including consolidation of peace, peace-building, and post-conflict reconstruction. In 1999, Japan's Overseas Economic Cooperation Fund (OECF) merged with the Export-Import Bank of Japan to form the new Japan Bank for International Cooperation. Information from Japan's Ministry of Foreign Affairs is available at www.mofa.go.jp.

anticipated that many more refugees would seek sanctuary there. PNG is a poor country and would be hard pressed to meet the needs of additional refugees. It suffers from many of the same problems as Papua, such as urban unemployment, environmental exploitation, and criminal activity. Some criminal enterprises, such as illegal logging, are known to operate on both sides of the border. PNG has its own experience with separatist violence. The Bougainville Revolutionary Army waged a ten-year war for independence from PNG during which 20,000 people were killed. The 2001 Bougainville Peace Agreement provided Bougainville with greater autonomy and pledged to conduct a referendum on independence within ten to fifteen years.

INTERNATIONAL ORGANIZATIONS

International organizations emphasize consensus decision-making and are typically wary of conflict-prevention initiatives. The Association of Southeast Asian Nations (ASEAN), which includes Indonesia, rarely criticizes a member state or takes a position on the internal affairs of one of its members. Since ASEAN lacks an intergovernmental conflict-prevention mechanism, concerns about conflict escalation are relegated to the ASEAN Parliamentary Forum.

While Indonesia may resist a political role by the UN in Papua, the UN Development Assistance Framework (UNDAF) incorporates preventive development strategies into the activities of specialized agencies (e.g., UNDP, the UN Children's Fund [UNICEF], the World Health Organization [WHO], the UN Population Fund [UNFPA], the UN Development Fund for Women [UNIFEM], and the UN Educational, Scientific, and Cultural Organization [UNESCO]). The "Partnership for Governance Reform" program, a national program supported jointly by UNDP, the World Bank, the ADB, and several bilateral donors, provides assistance to Indonesia in the area of good governance. Issues related to special autonomy are included in the scope of the partnership program.

The European Union (EU) finalized a "Conflict Prevention Assessment" on behalf of the European Commission (EC) Development

Cooperation Programme, focusing on good governance and sustainable natural-resource management. The 2002 report includes recommendations for strengthening the EU Rapid Reaction Mechanism. Though it criticizes the 1969 Act of Free Choice,[19] the EU prefers to avoid entanglements with the political issues associated with Papua's *merdeka* movement and instead focuses on good governance and sustainable development.

The Asia-Pacific Economic Cooperation (APEC) summit served as an important platform for mobilizing international attention during the East Timor crisis, primarily because violence in East Timor happened to coincide with the APEC annual meeting (September 1999). However, there is no other instance when APEC involved itself in a domestic conflict of a participating state. APEC has focused mainly on economic issues and has largely stayed away from politics. It has no coordinating mechanism for activities in between sessions.

While the Pacific Islands Forum was sympathetic to Papua's *merdeka* movement in the past, it adopted a resolution in August 2002 reaffirming its support for Indonesian unity. This initiative contradicts earlier efforts by Vanuatu, Nauru, and the Solomon Islands to champion Papua's independence and facilitate contacts for the Papua Presidium Council (PDP) at the United Nations. By diplomatically isolating the Free Papua Movement (OPM), the Pacific Islands Forum has sent a message endorsing mutual accommodation through Special Autonomy.

INTERNATIONAL FINANCIAL INSTITUTIONS

International financial institutions (IFIs) provided critical assistance to help Indonesia recover from the Asian financial crisis. Established in 1992, the Consultative Group on Indonesia (CGI) is chaired by the World Bank to coordinate financing among the CGI's 30 members (multilateral financial agencies and donor countries).

---

[19] Mawdsley et al., *Report of the EC Conflict Prevention Assessment Mission to Indonesia* (Brussels: EU, March 2002).

The World Bank has been active in Indonesia since 1967. It has provided $25 billion in the fields of economy, agriculture, education, health, social development, transport, energy, urban development, and infrastructure. The World Bank also provides technical assistance to economic policymaking, institutional development, and poverty alleviation. Since 1997, the World Bank has pledged $4.5 billion to Indonesia as part of an International Monetary Fund (IMF)–led assistance program. Under concessional terms, $500 million in International Development Association resources are provided annually. In addition, the World Bank has redirected another $1 billion into crisis-targeted programs (e.g., school scholarships, social and human development). At a World Bank conference on January 20, 2003, donors agreed to a $2.7 billion loan to help meet Indonesia's budget deficit and repay its debts. The World Bank links adjustment lending to policy reforms.

The International Monetary Fund leads efforts to promote macroeconomic stability in Indonesia. In February 2000, it launched a three-year, $5 billion arrangement to support economic and structural reform. The IMF's three-year program emphasizes development of a macroeconomic policy that supports recovery and entrenches price stability. The program seeks to reinvigorate banking, corporate governance, and other restructuring policies that are crucial to economic recovery and poverty reduction. Other goals include rebuilding key public institutions, strengthening capacity to implement economic and social policies, and enhancing transparency. Contingent upon program reviews and the achievement of performance targets, disbursements to date have been approximately $2.6 billion.

The Asian Development Bank (ADB) approved a $1.4 billion loan package following the onset of the Asian financial crisis in mid-1997. In 2002, the third and final tranche of this loan was disbursed via the Financial Governance Reform Sector Development Program. The release of these funds was postponed several times due to the delay by the Indonesian government in enacting fiscal controls. Despite difficulties in meeting anticorruption standards, Indonesia has been a member in good standing of the ADB since 1966. Indonesia is the fifth largest shareholder in the ADB among its regional members and is the sixth largest shareholder overall. In support of Indonesia's ongoing decentralization process, in December 2002 the ADB approved a loan of $42.22 million for capacity-building at the regional government level. In addition, the ADB will provide technical assistance, financed by a $1.2 million grant from the government of the Netherlands, for a separate monitoring system to review capacity-building implementation. The Sustainable Capacity Building for Decentralization Project will benefit 38–40 district governments.

Through the "Jakarta Consensus," donor countries to IFIs, such as the United States and the United Kingdom, could seek discussions about linking future financing with conflict-prevention criteria. It is unlikely, however, that Japan and other major donors would be supportive. Nor would private commercial and investment banks with positions in Indonesia (e.g., HSBC, ABN AMRO, and Citigroup).

As part of their overall financing approach, IFIs insist on macroeconomic structural reforms. The IMF's $5 billion Adjustment Lending Program includes performance targets and program reviews. The ADB's Financial Governance Reform Sector Development Program requires the government to enact fiscal controls, including a crackdown on corruption and money-laundering. However, no conflict-prevention criteria exist to condition financing by IFIs.

MULTINATIONAL CORPORATIONS

The U.S.-U.K. Voluntary Principles on Security and Human Rights focus specifically on building human rights safeguards into corporate security arrangements. The Voluntary Principles represent a first attempt at creating a corporate code of conduct in conflict situations. To operationalize the Voluntary Principles, a series of meetings involving corporations, officials from various embassies, and national government and Indonesian National Army (TNI) representatives was held in Jakarta (2001–2002). LEMHANAS (the National Defense Institute), a leading institution of higher education, has also convened meetings between companies and security-sector representatives to discuss international humanitarian law and the Voluntary Principles. Freeport and BP both subscribe to the Voluntary Principles. In addition, BP has incorporated the Voluntary Principles into its social and economic impact assessment for the Tangguh project in Papua; BP subcontractors must adhere to the company's Code of Conduct for Security Contractors.

A key objective of the Extractive Industries Transparency Initiative (EITI) is to achieve disclosure of the tax and non-tax payments (including royalties and signature bonuses) made to host governments, revenue authorities, and state-owned companies by oil, gas, and mining companies. The EITI aims to work closely with host governments and IFIs.[20]

In 1999, Freeport authorized a comprehensive Social, Employment, and Human Rights Policy. Two years later, it established the Voluntary Land Rights Trust Fund, which sets aside funds for descendants of the Amungme and Kamoro tribes residing near its project in Timika. Freeport made an initial payment of $2.5 million to the fund and has pledged annual payments of $500,000. In addition, Freeport's One Percent Fund provides $11 million to $18 million a year (i.e., 1 percent of the company's Papuan-derived gross revenues) for education, health, business, and infrastructure development. Freeport is also a part of the Global Mining Initiative, which seeks to mitigate negative social and environmental impacts from mineral extraction.

In partnership with BPMIGAS (Badan Pelaksana Migas), the Indonesian government petroleum-resource regulator, BP is developing the Tangguh Liquified Natural Gas Project, which will involve tapping the Tangguh fields, processing the gas into LNG, and shipping it primarily to East Asian markets, including China. British Gas, in collaboration with BP, will supply gas to the proposed Tangguh Liquified Natural Gas Project using reserves from production-sharing contracts for the Wiriagar, Berau, and

---

[20] Extractive Industries Transparency Initiative, www.dfid.gov.uk/News/News/files/eiti_guide.htm.

Muturi fields. BP is committed to socially and environmentally responsible resource development. It is working with local government and other partners to implement a diversified growth strategy (i.e., investments in regional towns). BP is also developing innovative community-based security arrangements.

INPEX is a Japanese-owned company that exports natural gas and supplies the Indonesian domestic market. In November 1998, INPEX acquired a 20 percent interest in Papua's East and West Arguni Blocks, of which BP owns the other 80 percent. JAPEX, owned by the government of Japan, works with BPMIGAS and controls 60 percent of the Semirak Block in Papua. Marubeni Sagindo is a Japanese company operating in Papua's forestry sector.

Other multinational corporations active in Papua include Conoco Phillips and Total Fina Elf, as well as Japanese, Korean, Australian, and other companies. Conoco has a 33-year operating history in Indonesia. It operates the Block B, Tobong, and Northwest Natuna Sea Block II production-sharing contracts and has an interest in South Sokang. In 1998, Pertamina and Sembawang Engineering and Construction finalized an agreement with the support of Conoco to sell 325 million cubic feet a day of natural gas to be transported via a new pipeline to Singapore. In partnership with BPMIGAS, Conoco is developing the offshore Belida oil field and the remote Block B gas fields. Total Indonesie (a subsidiary of Total Fina Elf), which is active in Kalimantan, also has interests in Papua's energy sector. Lasmo Runtu Ltd. controls the Runtu block encompassing the onshore Kutai Basin, where it has drilled five wells since 1990. Global SantaFe Corporation operates the Klamono oil field in Papua. Ramu International operates the Rombebai oil fields. Korea National Oil Company (KNOC) is a producer of both oil and gas. Mamberamo is an Australian company operating in Papua's forestry sector.

Nongovernmental Organizations

Development organizations in Papua have shown a willingness to discuss collaborative services and to coordinate their field operations for the purpose of maximizing donor contributions and avoiding competition for scarce grant resources. Among others, Catholic Relief Services, Oxfam Australia, and SIL International (formerly Summer Institute of Linguistics) serve as the implementing partners of official donors in Papua. Their field presence enables them to monitor funding streams from corporate revenue-sharing schemes, including the One Percent Fund.

Humanitarian organizations active in Papua include the International Catholic Migration Commission, Catholic Relief Services, and World Vision Australia. In addition to providing emergency assistance, these nongovernmental organizations (NGOs) emphasize humanitarian preparedness in the event of conflict escalation. Through its offices in Jakarta, the International Committee of the Red Cross (ICRC) organizes training programs for TNI on human rights and international humanitarian law.

The Papua Resource Center (PRC) is a new U.S.-based NGO with an advisory board of Papuan religious, educational, and cultural leaders. The PRC seeks to promote social welfare and indigenous culture in Papua by facilitating relationships between Papuan-based organizations and those in the international community with an interest in the region.

Transparency International is a world leader in addressing official corruption. It publishes the Global Corruption Report, which catalogs the performance of countries reducing corruption. In addition to monitoring, it provides technical assistance to official anticorruption efforts and capacity-building to local NGOs. Though it does not focus on Papua, Transparency International has offices in Jakarta.

The Open Society Institute is a worldwide network of foundations established by the New York–based financier George Soros. Its "Publish What You Pay" initiative encourages host governments to require major multinational corporations to disclose their balance sheets of overseas operations. In 2001, the OSI opened an office in Jakarta.

InterNews specializes in developing media institutions and news-reporting skills in television and radio for democracy education and civil-society building. In Papua, it supports radio stations and newspapers in a number of cities, while producing "Reporting for Peace" radio programs, which seek to cultivate a culture of peaceful resolution to local conflicts.

Conservation organizations active in Papua include the Center for International Forestry Research, the Australian Conservation Foundation, and the World Wildlife Fund. These groups work with local partners to monitor illegal logging and the illicit export of endangered species. Established by BP, the Tangguh Independent Advisory Panel is an independent body involved in a range of activities promoting the betterment of Papuans.

Conflict-prevention organizations working in Papua are Search for Common Ground, Catholic Relief Services, and World Vision Australia. The International Center for Transitional Justice, a leading international NGO with expertise in the areas of accountability and truth and reconciliation conducted in 2002 a mapping survey of reconciliation efforts in Indonesia.

GOVERNANCE

CONDITIONS (PAPUA)

Governance under President Suharto was characterized by virtual single-party rule, a strong nationwide security presence, and centralization of power and wealth. Basic social services for Papuans provided some benefits, but fell behind the rest of Indonesia, especially in Papua's rural areas. Many ethnic Papuans continued to rely for their basic needs on local systems of organization associated with churches and based upon *adat* (traditional modes of tribal and clan politics).

Following Suharto's departure, President B. J. Habibie addressed demands for more local governance by accepting plans for decentralization, called "Regional Autonomy" *(Otonomi Daerah)*. In 1999, President Habibie enacted this program through two laws (UU 22 and UU 25), which provided for local governments to keep an increased share of the wealth generated locally, while divesting a great deal of legislative and administrative powers to provincial and subprovincial bodies. As a further step toward local control of natural resources, the People's Legislative Council (DPR) passed legislation granting Special Autonomy for Papua *(Otonomi Khusus)*.

The Special Autonomy Law for Papua provides significant powers to the local government and guarantees cultural and religious rights to the people of Papua. It pledges 80 percent of local forestry, fishery, and mining revenues and 70 percent of income from oil and gas to local authorities.[21] The Special Autonomy Law also reaffirms traditional "customary law" and creates institutions to voice Papuan aspirations and promote indigenous rights. Special Autonomy liberalizes the formation of political parties,

---

[21] Mawdsley et al., *Report of the EC Conflict Prevention Assessment Mission to Indonesia* (Brussels: EU, March 2002).

creates village consultative bodies, and provides for the resolution of land conflicts via *adat* mediation.

The Special Autonomy Law calls for the establishment of a Papua People's Assembly (MRP). Drawing on the strength of *adat* political structures, the MRP is envisioned as an advisory body of tribal elders and church and women's leaders.

Officials at the regency level *(kabupaten)* anticipate large revenues. According to Papua's governor, Jaap Solossa, provincial income during the first year of implementation will increase threefold to around 2.5 trillion rupiah ($277 million) from 800 billion rupiah the year before. This total consists of 1.38 trillion rupiah from the "special autonomy allocation," another 400 billion rupiah from Jakarta under existing laws and local revenues of 770 billion rupiah.[22]

Implementation of Special Autonomy has been hindered by a heritage of mutual distrust, competing priorities in Jakarta, and lack of capability in Papua to handle increased responsibilities. To date, the MRP has not been formed due to disagreements over the scope of its authority. The anticipated increased local revenues have not been disbursed, nor have the devolutions of administrative responsibilities and authorities been completed.

Papua's governor, Solossa, with support from the speaker of the Provincial People's Legislative Council (DPRD), John Ibo, has been pushing Jakarta to implement Special Autonomy. In 2001, Solossa led Papuans in submitting a proposal to the national People's Legislative Council (DPR) to improve regulations governing the legislation.

Meanwhile, ethnic Papuans have been forming organizations of their own. Believing the Indonesian political process was not meeting their concerns, more than half of ethnic Papuans boycotted the 1999 general election.[23] The next year, more than 25,000 ethnic Papuans, including over 500 representatives of 253 tribes, and all major social, religious, and political organizations, gathered in the provincial capital of Jayapura to convene the Second Papuan

[22] International Crisis Group (ICG), *Al-Qaeda in Southeast Asia: The Case of the "Ngruki Network" in Indonesia* (Brussels/Jakarta: ICG, 8 August 2002).

[23] These estimates were supplied by Indonesian Election Watch.

Congress. That congress elected the 32-member Papua Presidium Council (PDP) to serve as an executive body. Since then, the PDP has stood as the single most widely accepted and inclusive entity representing the aspirations of ethnic Papuans. The Papuan Traditional Council (Dewan Adat Papua, or DAP) is a pan-Papuan tribal council, which is also emerging as a leading voice of the Papuan people

Though the PDP has tried to act as the single voice of ethnic Papuan aspirations, more radical groups do exist, such as the Koteka Tribal Assembly (DEMMAK) and guerrillas that consider themselves part of the Free Papua Movement (OPM) or the Papuan National Army (TPN). Most have recently abandoned their armed struggle and aligned with the PDP. Many Papuan political leaders demand "historical rectification" as an effort to set the record straight on Papua's accession into Indonesia, and to assert Papuan identity.

TRENDS

Decentralization is one of the most important reforms in Indonesia. The people of Papua are skeptical, as their previous experience with power-sharing has not been positive. Autonomy provisions were adopted in 1969 but never implemented. Some Jakarta-based interests see reform, democratization, and decentralization as a threat to national unity, and view revenue-sharing as a danger to their commercial interests.

A recent Presidential Instruction was adopted on the implementation of Law 45/1999, which divided Papua into three provinces (West, Central, and East Irian Jaya) (January 27, 2003). Though Jakarta originally issued the law dividing Papua into three provinces in 1999, it was never implemented. Law 21/2001 provides that any change in the composition of the province has to be considered by the Papua People's Assembly, a body that has not yet been formed. Most ethnic Papuans across the political and social spectrum oppose dividing Papua and see it as an effort to undercut Special Autonomy.

Many obstacles exist to implementing Special Autonomy. At the most basic level, government institutions in Papua are ill-equipped to handle the new responsibilities that would be expected of them, especially at the level of regencies and counties. Institutional deficiencies are likely to result in mismanagement, while also providing opportunities for manipulation and misappropriation. Implementing legislation has been passed in Jakarta for the purpose of refining the original laws, but it has often exacerbated confusion.

The Special Autonomy Laws for Papua and Aceh, adopted after decentralization legislation for the whole of Indonesia, devolved power to the provincial, not the regency *(kabupaten)*, level. Many central government departments are resisting requirements to divest power. Contradicting Law 21/2001, the Ministry of Forestry has recently stated that provincial governments will not be allowed to manage forest resources.

Another obstacle to implementing Special Autonomy at the local level is the lack of popular support among ethnic Papuans. Most believe they must choose between *merdeka* and *otonomi*. Given this choice, most ethnic Papuans would choose *merdeka*, which they see as a form of liberation. These sentiments discourage ethnic Papuans from supporting officially established institutions of governance. They rely primarily on *adat* and religious institutions as vehicles for political and social organization.

Ethnic strife is another important concern for Papua. Despite the announcement of Laskar Jihad's disbanding, there are continued concerns about conflict between ethnic Papuans and migrant groups, as well as between Papua's Christian and Muslim communities. Some Laskar Jihad members have relocated from the Malukus and are establishing operations near Papua's offshore energy sites and in the towns of Manokwari, Fak Fak, and Sorong. Plans are underway for an all-inclusive Papuan dialogue, as well as for a National Dialogue on Reconciliation.

OPTIMUM SITUATION

Full implementation of the Special Autonomy Law would represent a win-win situation for all parties. For this to happen, the people of Papua would see that Special Autonomy is about democratization, rather than a mechanism to foreclose the realization of their *merdeka* concept. Indonesian authorities would see that Special Autonomy is about satisfying the legitimate concerns of ethnic Papuans, rather than an interim step to political independence for a resource-rich part of the country. As stipulated in the authorizing legislation, maximum benefits would be realized by implementing Special Autonomy within two years, with implementation reviews proceeding within three years and every year after that.

Fully implemented, Special Autonomy would make the people of Papua feel that their safety and social welfare have improved. It would enhance educational opportunity for all Papuans and provide for their fair and equal representation in all walks of life, especially in the public sector. The people of Papua would also have their own flag, anthem, and constitution. Provincial authorities would play a role in negotiating transactions for future natural-resource development in Papua. Fully implemented, Special Autonomy would dramatically improve the lives of ethnic Papuans by increasing their standard of living and their sense that opportunity and justice exist within the context of Indonesia's national development. Positive advances would address many of the *merdeka* movement's deepest concerns. Winning the hearts of ethnic Papuans would dramatically improve stability.

RECOMMENDATIONS

To develop a legal and regulatory framework to support implementation of the Special Autonomy Law, the Commission recommends that

- The Indonesian government postpone any plan to divide Papua into three provinces and instead accelerate full implementation of the Special Autonomy Law. Any further action on the province's reorganization would be taken in consultation with the MRP.

- The Indonesian government establish the MRP and expand its role from an advisory group to the role specified in the Special Autonomy Law: a legitimate legislative body representing the *adat*, women's, and religious communities.

- The Indonesian government appoint a widely respected and experienced Indonesian as "Papua Coordinator." Assisted by national experts and international specialists in a "Special Autonomy Advisory Group," the Papua Coordinator would work with provincial authorities to draft laws and regulations required for implementing Special Autonomy.

- Stakeholder governments, international businesses, and non-governmental organizations (NGOs) make available specialists to serve on the Special Autonomy Advisory Group and provide training programs for officials in Papua.

To strengthen local capacity to implement Special Autonomy for Papua, the Commission recommends that

- The CGI work with national and provincial officials to assess and improve local capacity for improved governance, including management, budgeting, and administration.

- The UNDP, in coordination with the CGI, establish a "Papua Professional Corps" of national experts and international specialists sponsored by donor countries, international businesses, and NGOs to assist with social and economic development projects and to participate in the Special Autonomy Advisory Group.

- USAID provide additional resources targeting district government officials through its Performance-Oriented Management Program (PERFORM), and expand its legal reform program by further assisting the Indonesia Legal Aid Institute Foundation (YLBHI) in Papua.

To build popular support for Special Autonomy, the Commission recommends that

- USAID and other donors support a public-education program focusing on "democratization" and aimed at generating understanding and support for Special Autonomy.

- National and provincial authorities integrate legal bodies called for in the Special Autonomy Law with *adat* forms of adjudication and conflict resolution in keeping with Article 51 of the Special Autonomy Law.

- National and provincial authorities adopt legal reform, especially procedures for land claims in accordance with the Agrarian Law (UUD 1945).

- Provincial authorities develop a government oversight bureau ensuring fair and equal representation of ethnic Papuans in civil service.

THE ECONOMY

CONDITIONS (NATIONAL ECONOMY)

Indonesia has made progress from the low point of the financial crisis of 1997–98. Macroeconomic conditions have improved: Inflation is down; the rupiah is steady; and interest rates are reasonable. The budget deficit is less than anticipated. In addition, gross domestic product (GDP) is growing at a rate of 3 percent annually (2002), and the number of Indonesians living below the poverty line has decreased from 24 percent to 13 percent (1999–2002).

Despite progress, Indonesia's national economy is still plagued by high levels of debt, both external and domestic. Problems are compounded by a dearth of foreign investors and an overall loss of investor confidence. Foreign direct investment (FDI) has gone from $7 billion to $10 billion of new investment per year to the current situation, in which investors are withdrawing a net $2 billion to $3 billion per year. The deterioration of capital stock impedes equipment modernization, which, in turn, undermines economic performance and limits job opportunities. In addition, 40 percent of the total workforce of 100 million is unemployed or underemployed. More than half of the population survives on less than $2 a day. The Bali bombing has further set back prospects for the country's economic recovery by increasing perceptions of instability, while causing a loss of over $1 billion in tourist revenues.[24]

In February 2000, the International Monetary Fund (IMF) agreed to a new program that sought to restore GDP growth of 5 to 6 percent, lower annual inflation below 10 percent, decrease public debt to 65 percent of GDP by 2004, and eliminate "stand-bys" and other forms of special financing. The Indonesian Bank Restructuring Agency (IBRA) was established to deal with insolvencies in the financial sector.

---

[24] "Lured Back to Bali," *The Economist*, 6 February 2003, available at http://www.economist.com/displayStory.cfm?Story_ID=1567300.

Unfortunately, most performance goals adopted by Indonesia with encouragement by the IMF have not been achieved. In addition, government measures to eliminate corruption and enforce corporate transparency have not resulted in significant improvements in these crucial areas. On Transparency International's 2002 Corruption Perceptions Index, Indonesia ranked 96th out of 102 countries.[25] Nevertheless, legal reforms, which are key to improving these factors, remain sluggish. The sale of banks and corporations taken over by IBRA is proceeding slowly.

Of particular concern to Indonesia's immediate economic recovery are weak national policies and legislation governing petroleum and mineral extraction. Though Indonesia had done much to create a stable environment conducive to foreign investment in extractive industries beginning in the 1970s, recent years have seen a dramatic reversal of that trend—primarily due to ambiguous, onerous, and conflicting regulations at the national and regional levels. The current business milieu in Indonesia, particularly with respect to taxation and labor practices, discourages international and domestic investment. This phenomenon is particularly evident in the mineral sector. Though Indonesia ranks within the top one-third of mineral-rich nations of the world, it is currently receiving less than 0.9 percent of worldwide exploration dollars.[26] Without major improvements in these areas, Indonesia, and especially its resource-rich regions such as Papua, will soon lose a major part of its economic base. There will be a sharply decreasing stream of revenue to share.

CONDITIONS (PAPUA)

Papua's economy is dominated by natural-resource extraction, and as a result, land rights and natural-resource ownership are subjects of disagreement that often spark conflict. In addition, social

---

[25] Transparency International, *The 2002 Corruption Perceptions Index* (Berlin: Transparency International, 28 August 2002), available at www.transparency.org.

[26] *PricewaterhouseCoopers Mining Survey 2001.* See also the Fraser Institute, *Annual Survey of Mining Companies 2001/2002.*

tensions are exacerbated by the fact that local economies, including most retail businesses, are dominated by non-ethnic Papuan migrants. The government policy regarding natural-resource exploitation is based on Article 33 of the Indonesian Constitution, which states, "Land and water, and the natural resources found therein, shall be controlled by the state and shall be exploited for the maximum benefit of the people" (clause 3). Throughout Indonesia, the central government has granted resource-development rights to both national and foreign companies. These operations have contributed significantly to the Indonesian economy when viewed at the national, or macro, level. However, due to the tradition of centralization developed under the New Order, few economic benefits have flowed back to Papua. Though Papua contains some of Indonesia's most profitable natural resources, it is ranked above only West Nusa Tenggara in terms of poverty level by province in Indonesia.[27]

Most significant to the resource economy in Papua are the mining operations of PT Freeport Indonesia, the Indonesian subsidiary of Freeport-McMoRan Copper & Gold Inc. The company, which began operating in Papua in 1967, has since 1991 been mining the Grasberg ore body, the world's richest gold deposit and third richest copper deposit. This mine produces 222,000 tons of copper ore per day at the lowest cost in the world. The London-based multinational mining company Rio Tinto owns 13 percent of Freeport Indonesia and the Indonesian government is a 10 percent shareholder. As an index of its scale, and of its importance to the national economy, Freeport is Indonesia's single largest taxpayer (contributing an average of $180 million a year during the period 1991–2001), the largest employer in Papua, and the source of over 50 percent of Papua's GDP.[28]

Yet despite its massive contribution to the national economy, the economic effects of Freeport's operations at the local level have been mixed. Though Freeport has complied with government

---

[27] UNDP, *Human Development Report 2002*.

[28] Denise Leith, "Freeport's Troubled Future," *Inside Indonesia*, July–September 2001, available at www.insideindonesia.org/edit67/denise3.htm.

regulations regarding taxation, the national government's centralization has limited provincial-level benefits that might otherwise result from Freeport's operations. In a representative year, 1997, only $28 million, or 11.89 percent of the total taxes paid by Freeport, were disbursed to the provincial government.[29]

In response to widespread criticism, Freeport has made significant efforts to improve the local effects of its operations. An aggressive training and hiring program has increased employment of ethnic Papuans to 26 percent of Freeport's total workforce, although the number of Papuans in upwardly mobile and management positions remains extremely small. Nevertheless, though Freeport has invested $4.5 billion in the mine to date, relatively little of that investment directly affects the local economy. Infrastructure for its operations, such as in the company town Kuala Kencana, benefits mostly upper-level employees. Furthermore, salaries and other benefits paid to non-Papuans have little impact on the local economy, as employees send a large portion of their wages home. The vast majority of subcontractors is Jakarta-based and imports most of its supplies from outside Papua, including, for example, PT Pangansari Utama Food Industry, which feeds Freeport's massive workforce. Copper from Grasberg is shipped to and processed at the Gresik smelter in East Java, a $700 million joint venture between Freeport and Mitsubishi. There are sound business reasons for the awarding of these contracts, but from Papua's point of view, they may be missed opportunities.

Freeport has also made serious efforts to provide social services and improve the quality of life for those who live in the region of its operations. This has been an extremely difficult process, as the population around Freeport Indonesia's project site has exploded through spontaneous immigration and government-sponsored transmigration, increasing (by a factor of 10) to 110,000 persons in the last decade alone. In response, Freeport has initiated sev-

---

[29] Agus Sumule, "Protection and Empowerment of the Rights of Indigenous People of Papua (Irian Jaya) over Natural Resources under Special Autonomy: From Legal Opportunities to the Challenge of Implementation," Resource Management in Asia Pacific Working Paper No. 36 (2002).

eral reinvestment schemes and development programs,[30] the most significant being the One Percent Fund.[31] Founded in 1996 to last for ten years, the fund provides up to $18 million a year targeting education, health, business, and infrastructure development for seven Papuan tribes that occupy the greater area of Freeport's operations, including the Amungme and Kamoro who traditionally occupied the actual operation site. Unfortunately, management and distribution of this money has been contentious from the start. Though certain aspects of the fund, particularly health and education programs, have been somewhat successful, struggles over the fund's other uses have resulted in violent—even deadly—conflict on a number of occasions. Freeport has attempted to reform this fund by forming the Voluntary Land Rights Trust Fund, which places significant portions of the One Percent Fund in trust for Amungme and Kamoro descendants. In 1999, Freeport authorized a comprehensive Social, Employment, and Human Rights Policy.[32]

Totaling over 180 million hectares, Indonesia has the third largest expanse of tropical rain forest in the world.[33] Papua's forests alone cover approximately 41.5 million hectares, or 23 percent of Indonesia's total forested area. Of this, 27.6 million hectares of Papua are classified as "production forest,"[34] with nearly half of that area currently awarded to industrial foresters through concessions. The financial contribution of Papuan forestry to the central government has been approximately $100 million a year during the

---

[30] Freeport-McMoRan Copper & Gold, *Annual Report 2001*, p. 3.

[31] In April 1996, Freeport Indonesia agreed to commit at least 1 percent of its gross revenues for the next ten years to support village-based health, education, economic, and social development programs in its area of operations. Through the end of 2000, contributions to the fund have totaled approximately $92 million, including $80 million from Freeport Indonesia and $12 million from the company's joint venture partner in the Grasberg project, Rio Tinto.

[32] Freeport-McMoRan Copper & Gold, "Environmental and Social Program: Social, Employment, and Human Rights Policy," available at www.fcx.com/esp/socpolicy.html.

[33] Indonesia's tropical rainforest ranks third, behind those of Brazil and the Democratic Republic of the Congo. Global Forest Watch: Indonesia, www.globalforestwatch.org/english/indonesia.

[34] BPS Statistics Indonesia, www.bps.go.id/profile/irja.shtml.

past five years.[35] With the demand for timber continuing to grow, notably from China, and as forests in other parts of the country, including Kalimantan and Sumatra, are depleted, timber companies appear to be migrating to Papua.[36] Given that a majority of ethnic Papuans are in some way dependent on forest products for their livelihood,[37] forestry is a growing source of conflict, as exemplified by a major incident in Wasior in 2001 and ongoing problems in the Asiki District.[38]

Adding to the difficulties of managing the conflicts associated with forestry, the illegal logging business is thriving in Papua and across Indonesia. The national government estimates that trade in illegal logs costs the country $3 billion per year. Illegal logging does not comply with regulations regarding traditional landowner rights and in Papua is often pursued with protection from security forces, exacerbating tensions between state institutions and locals.

For decades, Pertamina has conducted a thriving oil business in Papua. Papua, however, is most significant as a site for potential growth in the petroleum industry. In 1997, Pertamina and Arco (later purchased by BP) embarked on a new project to develop the 24 trillion cubic foot Tangguh natural-gas field in the Bird's Head region of Papua (i.e., in the districts of Manokwari, Sorong, and Fak Fak). The fields will be operated by BP under a production-sharing contract with Pertamina. Liquefied natural gas (LNG) from Tangguh will be exported to China's Fujian Province.[39] Under the optimum situation, BP's revenues will begin to flow in 2010, after a four-year cost-recovery period, and will contribute $200 million to provincial and local authorities when the natural-gas fields

---

[35] The Indonesian Association of Forest Concession Holders (Asosiasi Pengusaha Huton Indonesia [APHI]), press release dated 2 March 2000.

[36] "Forests, People, and Rights," *Down to Earth Special Report,* June 2002, pp. 4–7.

[37] Agus Sumule, "Toward Sustainable Forest Management with Significant Participation of the Customary Communities in Papua, Indonesia," paper presented at the International Workshop on Sustainable Forestry Management, Bali, Indonesia, June 2001.

[38] *Indonesia Today: Daily News 2001,* available at www.indonesia-ottawa.org/Indonesiatoday/2001/feb01/020801.

[39] Keith Bradsher, "Australia Wins 25-Year Deal to Sell Gas to China," *New York Times,* 9 August 2002, p. W1.

reach peak production in 2015. Seventy percent of post-tax revenues will be divided between the provincial administration, which will retain 40 percent, and directly affected districts, which will receive 30 percent. The national government will receive the remaining 30 percent.[40] Though the initial construction workforce will be 5,000, it will decrease to 350 during regular operations.[41] On November 26, 2002, the United Nations Development Programme (UNDP) signed a memorandum of understanding (MoU) with the governor of Papua, local district heads, and BP, with witnessing signatures by the coordinating minister of economic affairs and the minister of settlements and regional infrastructure. The focus on UNDP's role in the MoU is to support and ensure management of a sustainable development plan for the Bird's Head region.

Though the resource sector clearly dominates Papua's economy at the macro level, the micro level also provides difficult problems to address from a conflict-prevention perspective. Much like large corporations engaged in natural-resource exploitation, small businesses throughout Papua are dominated by migrants, particularly from the islands of Sulawesi, Java, and Sumatra. Ethnic Papuans, who have been exposed to modern capital and cash economies for barely one generation in most cases, suffer from a severe lack of training and access to capital. The vast majority of Papuans remain marginalized from local economies, living a largely cashless existence of subsistence farming, gathering, and hunting. Increasingly this exclusion of Papuans from access to cash and commodities is a source of ethnic-based social tension throughout Papua.[42]

The primary crops cultivated differ by region but comprise sweet potatoes, taro, sago, and the areca nut. Butterfly sales constitute

---

[40] John McBeth, "Enlightened Mining Exploration: Irian Jaya," *Far Eastern Economic Review*, 27 December 2001.

[41] "For BP to Profit in Irian Jaya, Locals Must Profit, Too," *Asian Wall Street Journal*, 15 November 2001.

[42] A. Rumonsara and S. Kakisina, "The Indonesian Political Economy and Its Impact toward the Papuan People's Economy: Some Critical Issues to Be Considered in the Decentralization Era," paper presented in a roundtable focused on political and social development in Papua, Berlin, Germany, 29–30 June 2000.

an income for farmers in some regions and have resulted in the formation of farming groups to reduce competition and distribute benefits. Some local farmers have drawn on this experience and have organized rural extension cooperatives with export assistance from the Joint Development Foundation.

TRENDS

Uncertainty is bad for business, and there is a great deal of uncertainty in Indonesian national economic policies, in decentralization and revenue-sharing implementation, and in resource-extraction policies and practices. Nowhere is this climate of uncertainty more significant than in Papua. Prospects for implementation of current decentralization programs for Papua appear deeply compromised by overlapping and ambiguous regulations regarding the national decentralization program, Papua's Special Autonomy, and most dramatically, the recent Presidential Instruction regarding the division of Papua. This has caused tremendous uncertainty and confusion.

Closely linked to the Local Government Act (Law 22/1999), the Revenues Allocation Act (Law 25/1999) has given greater decision-making and financial power to all of Indonesia's regions. Under the national decentralization program, after excluding the share designated for Papua and Aceh, 25 percent of national domestic revenue is allocated to the provinces via the General Allocation Fund. Of this amount, 90 percent goes to districts and municipalities, with the remainder going to the provincial governments. Lack of transparency affects the flow of resources to regions nationwide, which was estimated at $6 billion in 2001.[43]

In addition to funds from the national General Allocation Fund, the Special Autonomy Law for Papua will channel 70 percent of oil and gas royalties and 80 percent of mining, forestry, and fishery royalties to the province. Changes to the new law appear

---

[43] SMERU Research Institute, *Regional Autonomy in Indonesia: Field Experiences and Emerging Challenges* (Bali, Indonesia: SMERU Research Institute, June 2002).

to have excluded national revenues from Freeport's corporate taxes. As compensation, for the next twenty years Papua is to receive an additional 2 percent of the General Allocation Fund that Jakarta distributes to the provinces, specifically earmarked for education, health, and infrastructure.[44] Papua will also receive a special appropriation for infrastructure development. The percentage to be redistributed from natural-resource exploitation will be reviewed after 25 years.[45] Although the applicable formulas are very complex and unclear at this time, it appears under the Special Autonomy Law that Papua will receive twice the amount it received as a result of the 1999 national decentralization program, or 700 trillion rupiah ($700 million).

The absence of a detailed plan for the transition process and the lack of supporting regulations have hampered effective implementation of Special Autonomy. Article 75 of the Special Autonomy Law stipulates that all implementing regulations must be enacted within two years of the law's adoption (November 21, 2001). Though distributions under Special Autonomy were supposed to have commenced in January 2002, it is not yet clear if and when Papuans will receive material benefits from the resource-sharing plan. On November 21, 2002, Jakarta announced plans for several bills to accelerate decentralization, but their effect is still to be determined.

Finally, the recent Presidential Instruction (January 27, 2003) dividing Papua into three provinces is likely to have dramatically adverse economic consequences, further discouraging foreign and domestic investment. Obstacles to investment associated with insufficiencies in the provincial government's administrative capacities and ambiguities regarding its jurisdiction and policies are quite significant in the current transition to Special Autonomy. Division of Papua at this time, before Special Autonomy has been effectively implemented, is effectively multiplying these obstacles by a factor of three.

[44] Ibid.
[45] Mawdsley et al., *Report of the EC Conflict Prevention Assessment Mission to Indonesia* (Brussels: EU, March 2002).

OPTIMUM SITUATION

Macroeconomic stability requires a comprehensive program of economic reform to expand the tax base and provide a favorable atmosphere for foreign investment. To reduce the overall debt-to-GDP ratio, IBRA would foreclose insolvent banks, vigorously recover assets, and hold primary shareholders accountable. Rapid sales of formerly private banks, linked with tax reform, would increase revenues to the national treasury, enabling it to better meet the budgetary requirements of government agencies.

In Papua, there is a direct link between economic development and conflict prevention. Measures would be adopted to expand the stake of the local population in the province's natural-resource development so that resource exploitation contributes to improving the living conditions of all Papuans. The Special Autonomy Law sets forth meaningful goals for equity and income-sharing. It would be fully implemented and efforts to increase the capacity of the people of Papua would be adopted.

In addition, national and multinational corporations operating in Papua can help by sustained and enhanced training and hiring of ethnic Papuans to share in economic benefits through affirmative-action employment preferences. They would also expand special compensation and more effectively deliver social services. Innovative financing schemes are needed for small and medium-sized businesses owned by ethnic Papuans, as are training and education programs that would foster professional skills and improve understanding of economic processes and opportunities. Transparent accounting and public reporting are needed to ensure that revenues returned to the province are as stipulated in the Special Autonomy Law.

RECOMMENDATIONS

To stimulate economic development resulting in more and better-paying jobs in Papua, the Commission recommends that

- International and national businesses sustain and enhance training and hiring of ethnic Papuans.

[58]

- National and provincial authorities apply funds made available to the province from revenue-sharing required by decentralization to support business training, microcredit, rural cooperatives, quick-impact projects, and employment-generation projects for ethnic Papuans.

- The Indonesian government arrange loans and grants from donors specifically targeting Papua.

To secure Papua's long-term economic future, the Commission recommends that

- The Indonesian government make foreign investment regulations more competitive at the national and provincial levels, particularly with respect to the resource industries of mining, forestry, and petroleum.

- National and provincial authorities prepare a province-wide master plan for sustainable resource development. Necessary expertise may be sought from stakeholder governments, international businesses, and NGOs.

- The Indonesian government include representatives of Papua in negotiations with non-Papuan businesses seeking to develop Papua's natural resources.

- The Indonesian government develop a special regional bank or enhance the capacity of province-owned banks to increase the availability of credit in Papua.

To promote transparency and counter corruption, the Commission recommends that

- National and provincial authorities sustain a campaign against corruption, including setup of an Anticorruption Commission in Papua.

- The Indonesian government, working with the Special Autonomy Advisory Group, develop procedures providing greater transparency of revenue transfers between businesses and central, provincial, and district governments per the "Publish What You

Pay" initiative,[46] requiring businesses to fully disclose tax and royalty payments.

- POLDA cracks down on illegal businesses that do not pay taxes.

- Donors support Papuan Chambers of Commerce to conduct seminars on corruption and business ethics.

- National and provincial authorities, in consultation with the CGI, arrange for Papua Professional Corps members to work in provincial government departments.

---

[46] On 13 June 2001, a coalition of 30 NGOs launched a worldwide appeal ("Publish What You Pay") to require oil, gas, and mining companies to publish net taxes, fees, and royalties and other payments as a condition for being listed on international stock exchanges. Available at www.publishwhatyoupay.org.

SECURITY

CONDITIONS (ARMED FORCES)

Following the collapse of Indonesia's parliamentary system and the declaration of martial law in 1957, the armed forces assumed an increasingly prominent role in the country's political and economic life. This role expanded on a 1950s doctrine called the "Middle Way" in what became known as the military's "dual function" *(dwi fungsi)*. Under *dwi fungsi*, in addition to defending external threats, the Indonesian National Army (TNI) acts as a "social and political force." President Suharto firmly established TNI as the primary guardian of the state, while at the same time consolidating his control and weakening potential challengers through general-officer appointments.

Like the rest of the country, TNI was galvanized by the crises and changes of 1997–98 to embark on a course of reform. Though the army was a critical element of support for the ruling GOLKAR party, it stood aside and allowed the fall of President Suharto and the conduct of free and fair elections in 1999. Subsequently, the army agreed to reduce its role in politics by relinquishing its reserved seats in all levels of the legislature by 2004. During the 2002 debate on constitutional reforms, TNI played a key role opposing the imposition of shari'a (Islamic law), which would have gone some distance toward making Indonesia an Islamic state. TNI also acceded to being divested of the Indonesian National Police (POLRI), which was placed under the direct command of the president. For the first time since the 1950s, Indonesia has a civilian as minister of defense, albeit with limited powers. Beginning in 2000, TNI lost much of the country's esteem, though more recently it has regained some of the lost ground.

The army has adamantly resisted proposals to fully dismantle its Territorial Command Structure (KODAM), through which it is involved in civilian government functions. Formal army doctrine called for "ensuring the security and success of each government program in the field of development" and "the stabilization of social conditions to generate the basis for national development and security." Reflecting the traditional belief that the primary danger to the nation is not external aggression but internal subversion, KODAM was created as a structure of control paralleling the civilian government, hypothetically reaching down to every village. Though it has been greatly reduced from pre-1998 levels, the KODAM structure still enables the army to retain influence in political and economic affairs.

It has proven much more difficult for TNI to disengage from its commercial activities. In 2001, the national budget allocated $1 billion to TNI, only 25–30 percent of its total costs.[47] Funding allocated for Indonesia's military is less than that of the militaries in Singapore ($4.4 billion), Thailand ($2 billion), the Philippines ($1.3 billion), and Malaysia ($1.6 billion). TNI soldiers are poorly paid, with mid-ranking soldiers earning $60 to $95 per month and high-ranking officers earning $110 to $350 per month.[48] Their income compares unfavorably with the salary structure of comparable professionals in Indonesia. Members of the military rank and file are forced to engage in other income-generating activities in order to meet the basic needs of their families.

TNI meets its own budget gap by generating other revenues, such as by operating an array of commercial enterprises (e.g., airlines, hotels, banks, and insurance companies). TNI's tax-exempt charitable foundations *(yayasan)* are linked to holding companies, whose for-profit business activities funnel money back to the foundations to subsidize welfare activities (e.g., housing, schools, and medical facilities). In addition, TNI operates local cooperatives, which provide basic necessities to troops at subsidized rates. State-owned corporations, such as Pertamina and Bulog, pay TNI to support project security costs. TNI also derives income through

---

[47] "Back to Barracks," *The Economist*, 17 August 2002, p. 34; and Stanley A. Weiss, "Send the Military to Business School," *International Herald Tribune*, 19 September 2002, p. 6.

[48] "Indonesian Soldiers among Worst Paid in Asia, Laments Army Chief," Agence France Presse, International News, 26 June 2002.

unofficial taxes on local business, informal commercial ventures, and illicit activities.

TNI is seeking to address calls for greater transparency by complying with the Criminal Corruption Law (31/1999), which stipulates that *yayasan* funds should also be categorized as state finance and subject to audit by the Supreme Audit Agency (Badan Pemeriksan Keuangan). The process of auditing foundations was initiated in May 2000. Though questions were raised about the accounting practices of the army's largest foundation, Yayasan Kartika Eka Paksi, the fact that a civilian agency is auditing a military foundation represents progress toward the financial accountability of TNI.

TNI's performance of its internal security duties has ranged from very progressive, professional, and effective to disorganized, brutal, and counterproductive. Many TNI commanders believe that their role as guardians of national unity requires and justifies ruthless action against individuals and groups suspected of independence sentiments. For the same reason, TNI leaders resent and resist accountability for their own and their soldiers' actions outside the military legal system, which has shown little impartiality. Inadequate TNI budgets often result in the sending of poorly trained troops to establish security in areas of sectarian violence and independence movements. The results are predictable. Inadequate budgets also open field units to manipulation and corruption from outside the chain of command.

This combination of inadequate resources and training, vulnerability to corruption, and ruthless action to preserve national unity has caused a pattern of TNI actions damaging property, dealing brutally with civilians, and causing unaccounted-for deaths in many areas of Indonesia, including Papua. Reforms have had some effect, but the performance of TNI troops assigned to security duties does not yet meet international expectations for the armed forces of democratic governments.

In Papua, there are approximately 8,000 TNI troops, including Special Forces (KOPASSUS) and three Strategic Reserves Command (KOSTRAD) battalions. TNI has a significant presence near the Freeport mine in Timika. In 1996, Freeport paid the armed forces a one-time fee of $35 million for its security assistance. It also agreed to make an annual contribution of $11 million to TNI.[49] All Indonesian oil and gas production-sharing agreements, including BP's, require the partner company to subsidize security expenses mandated by BPMIGAS, the government petroleum-resource regulator. Production companies advance all security costs and then deduct BPMIGAS's share from project revenues. As an alternative, BP is emphasizing community-based security.

As they do in forested regions throughout the country, individual TNI units and officers also profit from illegal logging in Papua.[50] These activities are undertaken both as small-scale "poaching" and through institutional relationships with Indonesian companies such as the Jayanti Group and foreign firms such as Korea's PT Korindo. In a positive development, Commander General Sutarto of TNI condemned these activities and announced plans to curb illegal logging by soldiers. TNI involvement in the trade of endangered species indigenous to Papua has also come to light.

CONDITIONS (POLICE)

The Indonesian National Police was originally merged into the armed forces by President Suharto. In 1999, President B. J. Habibie removed POLRI from the Ministry of Defense and planned to assign it to the Interior Ministry. Before this was implemented, President Abdurrahman Wahid elevated POLRI to a separate and independent command under the direct control of the president. The separation of TNI and POLRI was encouraged by the U.S. government as a prerequisite to launching the International Criminal Investigative Training and Assistance Program (ICITAP) for the national police. Ongoing competition between the

---

49 Frida Berrigan, *Indonesia at the Crossroads: U.S. Weapons Sales and Military Training* (New York: World Policy Institute, October 2001).

50 "US May Support a Terrorist-Connected Military in Name of War on Terror" (Washington, D.C.: Peace Action, 2002).

army and the police over patronage and revenues still complicates the task of delineating their roles and responsibilities. Open conflicts are common. Tensions recently flared in northern Sumatra on September 29, 2002, when a TNI battalion attacked a police post after local police refused to release a civilian friend of TNI who had been detained for drug possession. The Special Autonomy Law, which shifts authority for law enforcement to provincial governments, has further exacerbated difficulties between TNI and POLRI.

POLRI's resource requirements were a low priority when it was subordinated to TNI. Funding has not improved since TNI and POLRI were separated. Police officers are poorly trained and equipped; personnel are underpaid and poorly housed. They are dissatisfied, demoralized, and lacking motivation. Such conditions breed corruption and, in turn, engender dislike, distrust, and fear of the POLRI by the communities they serve. A recent public-opinion poll on corruption in public institutions rated the police at the bottom of all government agencies. At the same time, POLRI is much more decentralized than is TNI. Through the Provincial Police (POLDA), the police force has historically contained a significant percentage of the local population. For this reason, the police tend to be better integrated and more accepted into local communities than military units.

In addition to difficulties fulfilling its domestic security role, POLRI has limited intelligence-gathering and analytic capabilities. Its inadequacies were glaring in a number of high-profile cases, including that of the fugitive Tommy Suharto and that surrounding the bombings of churches and office buildings in Jakarta. Unskilled crime-scene procedures have heightened concerns about the ability of POLRI to conduct a credible investigation or, most significantly, to address Indonesia's growing terrorist threat. Despite initial local bungling at the Bali bomb site, the police, aided by international experts, have been remarkably successful in arresting members of the terrorist group responsible and confiscating weapons, explosives, and support equipment.

It will take a long time to transform POLRI into a competent and professional force. In the aftermath of Bali, international donors are showing keen enthusiasm to support the police. At the same time, their neglect of the armed forces is exacerbating tension and fueling competition for resources. Increasing incidents of violence are occurring between TNI and POLRI.

In Papua POLDA numbers 8,700—of which 1,300 are ethnic Papuans—a much larger percentage of local involvement than is seen in TNI in Papua. Papuan police forces include the Police Special Forces (GEGANA) and the Mobile Brigade (BRIMOB). Centrally controlled by POLRI in Jakarta, these units are the best-armed and most combat-capable elements in the police force. Much like TNI's KOPASSUS, BRIMOB is accused of human rights abuses and involvement with criminal activities.

CONDITIONS (MILITIAS)

A wide assortment of violent, if poorly armed, militias are active in Papua. Some of these militias, such as the youth group Pemuda Pancasila and the Islamic radicals of Laskar Jihad, operate in other provinces as well. Though Laskar Jihad has formally announced that it is disbanding, reports from Papua suggest otherwise.

The most significant militia network in Papua is the so-called Free Papua Movement (OPM) that includes between 10 and 20 loosely organized and occasionally competing groups scattered throughout the province, especially in forested areas on the outskirts of population centers.

The OPM appears to have made occasional strikes against Indonesian security forces. However, there are reports that some OPM groups have covert symbiotic relationships with TNI units. Pro-Indonesian militias, called the Barisan Merah Putih (Red and White Brigade), are organizing along the border with Papua New Guinea and appearing more and more near Papua's western population centers.

Report

TRENDS

The historical record of security-force activities in Papua includes a heavy-handed crackdown against alleged independence sympathizers and minimal accountability for crimes against Papuans. Recent TNI reforms and improvements in training have not fundamentally changed this pattern.

Under the leadership of I Made Mangku Pastika, the respected former POLDA police chief, and his replacement Budi Utomo, investigations into the murder of PDP Chairman Theys Eluay have been pursued with unprecedented vigor. Their reassignment from the investigation raises concern that progress may be jeopardized. TNI's parallel investigations have not been as effective or as forthcoming. Though seven KOPASSUS soldiers were convicted of killing Theys Eluays, there has been no attempt to fix responsibility up the chain of command for the command influence—if not the specific orders—that led low-ranking soldiers to physically assault, and kill, the prominent Papuan leader. An additional POLDA report suggested that TNI was behind the killings in Tembagapura of two Americans and an Indonesian teacher working for Freeport. These reports and the recent dismissal of police investigating the case have further exacerbated tensions between the military and police. Meanwhile, TNI security patrols in remote regions still routinely use harassment and violence to intimidate Papuans. No senior military personnel have been called to account.

The 2003 U.S. defense appropriation includes $17.9 million for regional training, including $4 million for training the military in Indonesia. The homeland defense supplemental appropriation provides $16 million for law enforcement and counterterrorism training of Indonesia's police. The foreign operations appropriation proposes $400,000 in International Military Education and Training Program (IMET) funds for Indonesia. In addition, Indonesian officers have been invited to attend a fifteen-month counterterrorism workshop at the U.S. Naval Postgraduate School in California.

Examples of international donor assistance for security-sector reform include the programs of the Australian Agency for International Development (AusAID) and the U.S. Department of Justice's International Criminal Investigative Training and Assistance Program (ICITAP), a five-year effort to transform POLRI into a civilian police agency committed to democratic practices and human rights. Through ICITAP, POLRI is participating in courses on democratic policing, community policing, and police ethics. A pilot training program in civil-disturbance management is also being developed. In addition to ICITAP's training in proper police procedures, the International Committee of the Red Cross (ICRC) offers courses in ethics, international humanitarian law, and human rights. Despite these efforts, reform will take many years given the deeply engrained attitudes of the military and its "reform fatigue."

Though various militia groups continue to operate in Papua, their importance is diminishing due to strong civilian opposition and efforts by POLRI to adopt more robust measures enforcing domestic security. Suharto's Pemuda Pancasila, which was accused of atrocities in East Timor, is allegedly involved in drugs, prostitution, and extortion in Papua. Other militias include the Red and White Brigade and Laskar Jihad, a Muslim fundamentalist paramilitary group with strong anti-Western views. In response to the arrival of Laskar Jihad in Papua, local religious leaders of all faiths have banded together to reject "outside provocateurs."

U.S. Actions Involving TNI and POLRI

U.S. support to and interaction with TNI have played a prominent role in overall U.S. policy toward Indonesia.

The U.S. Congress curtailed military cooperation, effectively ending IMET, after TNI was implicated in the East Timor Santa Cruz massacre (November 12, 1991). IMET pays for the training of foreign military personnel on topics ranging from counterintelligence to military justice. Expanded IMET (E-IMET) was substituted for IMET during this period. E-IMET supports noncombat courses with an aim of increasing awareness about internationally recognized human rights. President Bill Clinton froze all military assistance and cooperation after TNI was implicated in razing East Timor following its vote for independence (September 1999). Since then there has been limited cooperation, including joint humanitarian exercises, sale of nonlethal spare parts, and continuation of E-IMET.

U.S. Secretary of State Colin Powell has stated that restrictions on military cooperation have diminished America's ability to influence the new generation of TNI leaders. To strengthen the case for resuming military cooperation, Secretary Powell hopes for "something serious on the accountability front to indicate that the Indonesian military is really on the road to reform."[51] So far, however, Indonesia has not demonstrated enough progress to justify resumption of substantial expanded cooperation.

Since September 11, the United States has provided training and other assistance to POLRI, to improve both counterterrorism capabilities and overall competence. The Federal Bureau of Investigation (FBI) is working with TNI and POLRI to investigate the killings in Tembagapura. Eight other Americans were wounded in that attack.

OPTIMUM SITUATION

Reformed, competent, accountable security services are essential for a democratically developing Indonesia. At the national level, it will take a major effort, involving not only TNI and POLRI but also the president and the legislature. The major elements of reform are

- Establishing external defense and the protection of national sovereignty as TNI's primary mission, and reducing TNI's internal security function to a backup role to POLRI, including a reorganization of KODAMs to confine their role to purely military functions.

---

[51] "U.S., Indonesia Starting to Normalize Military Ties," Embassy of the United States of America to Indonesia, 5 August 2002.

- Focusing the military on external threats through a more mobile, better-trained, and better-equipped army, and strengthening the ability of the Indonesian Marines, Navy, and Coast Guard to interdict smuggling and piracy and of the Air Force to perform surveillance of Indonesia's territorial waters and airspace.

- Resuming TNI's traditional respected participation in international peacekeeping missions, particularly in Muslim countries.

- Providing adequate national budgetary support to TNI and POLRI, thereby eliminating the need and justification for involvement in commercial or illegal activities.

- Establishing regular independent audits of TNI income and expenditures throughout the country and at every level of the armed forces.

- Professionalizing the TNI officer corps and police forces by providing better training and improving pay, housing, medical care, and education for officers and their dependents.

- Establishing full control of TNI and police forces and implementing accountability systems.

- Ending exclusive military jurisdiction over "areas of vital national interest" and transferring these areas to control by the police and civilian authorities.

There are no quick solutions, even with strong leadership both within and outside TNI. Indonesia's huge debt and large current budget deficit make expanded budgetary support for TNI unlikely in the short term. Donors such as the United States, Australia, and the European Union (EU) member states should monitor TNI's progress and assess reforms. Providing a pool of funds for military assistance and reform measures would provide needed resources and avoid the politicization of bilateral programs. In addition to documenting TNI's human rights performance, an informal "report card" could be used by the World Bank Consultative

Group on Indonesia (CGI) to consider the effect of its assistance on realizing reforms, and as a basis for considering future assistance to TNI.

The Commission is strongly in favor of actions by both the United States and other stakeholder nations to encourage and support these reforms for TNI and POLRI. Those actions include

- Stakeholder governments expanding education and training programs that teach the principles and practices of armed forces in democratic countries (e.g., democracy transition training and senior leadership seminars).

- Carefully calibrated resumption of other forms of military assistance as Indonesia makes progress on the reform agenda of TNI.

Papua cannot wait, however, for the completion of a comprehensive national security–sector reform program. In Papua, better-trained, adequately paid, and more accountable security forces are essential to providing necessary law, order, and security while decreasing resentments that fuel pro-independence sentiment.

In Papua, the repressive approach of the security forces is increasingly counterproductive; rather than decreasing Papuan support for independence, these measures are increasing pro-independence sentiments. Repressive measures are also stirring international attention to and sympathy for Papuan independence.

RECOMMENDATIONS

To improve the capability, performance, and accountability of security forces in Papua, the Commission recommends that

- The Indonesian government and TNI place tight limits on the activities of KOPASSUS in Papua and, over time, remove KOPASSUS from Papua.

- Donors of military and police assistance develop programs, in conjunction with TNI and POLDA, concentrating advisory and training activities on units in Papua, and focusing on effective security procedures that respect citizens' rights and emphasize community-based policing.

- The Indonesian government allocate some decentralization revenues for the education, housing, and health care of TNI and POLDA personnel and their families.

- TNI and POLDA follow up recent successes cracking down on illegal logging by further reducing involvement of personnel in illicit activities.

To strengthen the role of the police, the Commission recommends that

- POLRI continue its responsibility for law and order, including reformulating the mandate and mission of BRIMOB to strictly conform with regular police activities.

- POLRI enforce requirements that BRIMOB and GEGANA report directly to the POLDA police chief in Jayapura.

- POLDA continue to expand the number of ethnic Papuan police so that local police forces reflect the ethnic composition of the communities they serve.

- The U.S. government boost aid through ICITAP; provide more assistance to the National Police Academy; and expand the police-training assistance team with emphasis on training in police procedures (e.g., investigations, forensics, and bomb disposal).

To engage multinational corporations in helping to improve security procedures, the Commission recommends that

- The Indonesian government revise the law on the protection of national assets to end the requirement that businesses use TNI for security contracts, so that private local security organizations can be developed.

- International businesses promote "community-based security" as a new approach to project security once the law on the protection of national assets is changed.

- International businesses consult with local communities on security concerns and requirements through local committees involving TNI, POLDA, tribal leaders, and *adat* institutions.

- International businesses operating in Papua gradually phase out their security-service contracts with TNI, as changes in Indonesian law permit, and report on their compliance with the "Voluntary Principles on Security and Human Rights."[52]

---

[52] The U.S. and U.K. governments facilitated a dialogue among companies from the extractive sector, human rights organizations, and corporate social-responsibility groups. The goal was to develop guidance on how companies operating in zones of conflict should deal with providing protection to their employees without becoming involved in human rights violations. The Voluntary Principles were announced on 20 December 2000 and lay out the criteria for assessing the risks of such violations and provide guidance for the relationship between the company and public and private security forces.

SOCIAL DEVELOPMENT

CONDITIONS

Ethnic Papuans are trapped between their traditional isolation and the compelling forces of modernity. Today, economic development and changing demographics are exposing ethnic Papuans to the outside world and accelerating Papua's modernization. Most ethnic Papuans are estranged by these changes, which are gradually eroding traditional institutions and values.

Papua's isolation was largely uninterrupted during Dutch colonial rule. Even by the end of the 1950s, only a handful of Christian missionaries had made contact with Papua's traditional agrarian communities. Since 1969, migration has altered Papua's demographics and stirred social conflict. Of Papua's 2.1 million people,[53] there are approximately 800,000 migrants.[54] Migrants are concentrated in cities, where they dominate economic activities and the civil service.[55] Papua is divided between the migrant western Indonesians and the ethnic Papuans, who have distinct cultural characteristics.

Papuan identity was preserved through informal systems of local organization associated with the churches and based upon *adat*. Most ethnic Papuans are Christians and have strong affiliations with Protestant and Catholic churches. The Indonesian Islamic Council also has an active chapter in Papua that includes both migrants and ethnic Papuans. In addition to their spiritual purpose, religious institutions provide a wide variety of services, including health care, education, and civil-society mobilization, especially of women's groups.

---

[53] BPS Statistics Indonesia, "Indonesia's 2000 Population Census," Bangkok, 29 November 2000. The total population of Papua was estimated at 2,112,756. Because of the "unstable situation" in Papua, the enumeration was carried out "only in areas with condusive situations for census undertaking."

[54] Information provided by the UNDP in Jakarta.

[55] "Indonesia: Ending Repression in Irian Jaya."

With funding from foreign governments and private donors, nongovernmental organizations (NGOs) have become political forces with talented young people active in both service delivery and advocacy.

Just as the fall of President Suharto opened space for political and civic activity, it also created opportunities for free expression. Dozens of magazines, tabloids, and newspapers have sprung up in Papua. Given the limited literacy of the people of Papua, radio is an extremely popular medium. Funded by the U.S. Agency for International Development (USAID), InterNews backs two private radio stations in Jayapura. Radio Republik Indonesia operates ten stations in Papua.

Papua's educational infrastructure is incapable of servicing the province's predominantly young population (40 percent of which is under age 14).[56] The majority of ethnic Papuans have received either no schooling or a limited amount of grammar school. The literacy rate for women is 44 percent, compared to 78 percent in the rest of Indonesia, and, for men, 58 percent compared to 90 percent nationwide.[57] Low levels of education exist despite the existence of 2,378 elementary schools, 238 junior high schools, and 105 senior high schools.[58] Only 10 percent of the people of Papua have a high school education and only 1 percent has graduated from college.[59]

The Indonesian government operates both national and village schools. The curriculum is conducted in Bahasa Indonesia, the national language. Some schools are geographically so remote that teaching materials are slow to be delivered and are often inade-

---

[56] Stephanus Kakisina, "Development in the Land of Papua, For Whom?" paper submitted to the roundtable on the issues of human rights in Papua, at the Orville H. Schnell, Jr., Center for International Human Rights, Yale Law School, New Haven, Conn., 25 March 2002.

[57] U.S. Department of State, Bureau of East Asian and Pacific Affairs, "Background Note Indonesia," October 2000; University of Texas, "West Papua Information Kit"; UNDP, *Human Development Report 2002; Irian Jaya Dalam Angka 1998* (Badan Pusat Statistik Irian Jaya, 1999).

[58] "National Education Minister Opens Papuan University," *Jakarta Post*, 6 January 2001.

[59] Kakisina, *Development in the Land of Papua, For Whom?*

quate when they arrive, if they arrive at all. School buildings are dilapidated and neglected. Most primary schools lack facilities, furniture, and material support. Budget limitations affect the provision of learning materials and basic salaries for educational personnel. Teacher qualifications are low, especially in remote village schools. Some poorly trained teachers are paid even though they do not show up for work, while many good teachers are never paid. Educational opportunities are much more significant at schools that receive grants from Freeport. Churches sponsor some 30 private schools and universities. International NGOs, including SIL International, are training teachers and providing schoolbooks.

The health sector suffers from the same neglect and inadequate resourcing as does education. Papua has only three hospitals, including one sponsored by Freeport. Every subregency is required to have a clinic *(puskesmas)*, but these are poorly staffed and underequipped. Over 20 percent of the population in the central highlands suffer from malnutrition and vitamin deficiencies. Over 50 percent of children less than five years old are undernourished, and infant mortality is more than double that of Indonesia as a whole. In addition, the maternal mortality rate is three times greater in Papua than in the rest of Indonesia. Only 40.8 percent of children are immunized, compared with a national average of 60.3 percent. Inadequate primary health care results in fatalities from preventable diseases. Of infant deaths, 26 percent are caused by pneumonia, 19 percent by diarrhea, and 11 percent by malaria.[60]

Average life expectancy for the people of Papua is 40–50 years (i.e., 15 years less than the national average).[61] Many women participate in coercive official family-planning programs, but little is done to prevent sexually transmitted diseases. Ignorance, stigma, and discrimination are allowing the transmission rate of the

---

[60] U.S. Department of State, Bureau of East Asian and Pacific Affairs, "Background Note Indonesia"; University of Texas, "West Papua Information Kit"; UNDP, *Human Development Report 2002*; New Internationalist 344, West Papua: The Facts, April 2002.
[61] Ibid.

human immunodeficiency virus/acquired immune deficiency syndrome (HIV/AIDS) to increase rapidly. Statistics in this area are unreliable and cases underreported. There are 1,125 currently registered cases of HIV/AIDS in Papua,[62] 80 new cases are reported every month, and the official HIV/AIDS rate in Papua is now almost 30 times the national average. From 1990 to 1995, the number of cases tripled, with the highest incidence near a prostitute village in Timika. It is feared that as many as 5 percent of Papua's population is already infected.[63]

To enhance social and economic development, USAID has classified Papua as one of its six priority provinces in Indonesia. Official development assistance is augmented by contributions from international businesses which, in the case of Freeport, channel funds to communities directly affected by their operations. Freeport designates 1 percent of its gross revenues to community development. Its One Percent Fund supports services, education, infrastructure, and microfinance projects. BP's contributions will eventually be comparable; presently, BP contributes $6 million to USAID's Global Development Alliance. Despite these efforts, Papua is ranked as Indonesia's second poorest province by the 2002 UNDP Human Development Index.[64]

TRENDS

The largest impact of the Special Autonomy Law for Papua is the proposed redistribution of revenues to local authorities. If these funds are disbursed, and the provincial government applies them in the service of social development, Special Autonomy will have a significant impact on the people of Papua. The law also strengthens traditional social institutions, reaffirms traditional customary

---

[62] Antara Interactive, "HIV/AIDS Cases in Papua Cause for Great Concern," 2 October 2002, available at www.antara.co.id/e_berita.asp?id=48088.

[63] Chris W. Green, "Spread of AIDS in Papua at Alarming Level," *Jakarta Post*, 3 October 2002. See also Aksi Stop AIDS, www.fhi.org/en/cntr/asia/indonesia/indonesciahv/indonesiahvofc.html.

[64] UNDP, *Human Development Report 2002*.

law, and creates institutions to voice Papuan aspirations and promote indigenous rights. It creates village consultative bodies and provides for the resolution of land conflicts via traditional mediation mechanisms.

Increasing ethnic and religious rivalries represent the greatest threat to social cohesion in Papua. Religious leaders from many faiths have responded by becoming involved in interreligious dialogues. For example, the Working Group between Religions (Kelompok Kerja Antar Agama) has been organized by the Jayapura Diocese of the Catholic Church and is working to avert interreligious conflict. In addition, the media are increasingly used to promote conflict resolution. InterNews is producing "Reporting for Peace" radio programs, which seek to cultivate a culture of peaceful resolution to conflicts.

Despite Freeport's community-development efforts, some Papuans believe the company has exacerbated social tensions and degraded the natural environment. Grasberg mine tailings and waste have polluted rivers and eroded the soil. The bulk of Freeport's assistance acts as a "humanitarian magnet," drawing displaced populations to Timika and primarily benefiting migrant populations. Distribution is geographically uneven. *Adat* and local leaders are not adequately consulted.

OPTIMUM SITUATION

A vibrant civil society with trust between citizens and government organizations is needed to ensure that Papuans derive the maximum possible benefit from Special Autonomy. Civil-society participation would also create confidence among the people of Papua that Special Autonomy will result in measurable benefits to their quality of life. Without a strong civil society, illegal activity will grow and corrupt officials will steal revenues or direct funds to cronies or followers. Civil society can help law-enforcement organizations curtail illicit activities, such as illegal logging and trade in endangered species, by frowning on and reporting specific cases.

Better schooling and health care would reverse the trend of marginalization. As a starting point for improving the education sector, a comprehensive assessment would be undertaken of infrastructure, accessibility, qualifications, teacher-student ratios, retention rates, curriculum, and language of instruction. Discussions about improving education would involve teachers, families, and other civil-society representatives. Primary health care and women's health are priorities. Improved environmental protection is needed in urban areas and near development projects. Traditional forms of mediation and conflict prevention are essential to maintaining social order and realizing more harmonious interethnic and interfaith relations.

By working in tandem with international donors and multinational corporations, civil-society groups can use their access to communities across the province to improve humanitarian conditions. *Adat* institutions and church groups, whose respect is unparalleled at the grassroots level, are essential service providers and hubs for community organizing. In addition, multinational corporations would adjust their reinvestment and community development programs to benefit rural residents. *Adat* institutions would be consulted and synergies sought with official development assistance.

RECOMMENDATIONS

To strengthen civil-society institutions in Papua, the Commission recommends that

- The Indonesian government use church and women's groups to augment delivery of health and education services.

- Donors and the Indonesian government support local civil-society organizations, *adat* institutions, and human resource development.

- Donors and the Indonesian government support civil-society organizations that seek to guard against corruption in the private and public sectors, and organizations that monitor decentralization and Special Autonomy.

- Donors support the interfaith cooperation movement of Kelompok Kerja Antar Agama and the peace movement (the Peace Commission for Papua).

- The U.S. government increase the number of Papuans participating in Fulbright scholarships to study overseas and expand the International Visitors Program to include more Papuans.

To improve Papuan education and bring standards in line with conditions elsewhere in Indonesia, the Commission recommends that

- The Indonesian government work with UN agencies and donors to conduct an assessment of the education sector (schools, facilities, staff, etc.).

- The Indonesian government work with the UN Children's Fund (UNICEF), the UN Educational, Scientific, and Cultural Organization (UNESCO), and donors to overhaul the education system by

  - Paying teachers using funds from decentralization.

  - Eliminating school fees and implementing school-lunch programs.

  - Developing preschools through the network of women's groups; supporting the establishment of more private and church-run colleges and technical schools; and highlighting the importance of education through a public-awareness campaign undertaken by church and women's groups.

  - Expanding informal educational opportunity in remote villages by working with church and women's groups to expand educational outreach (e.g., via small community libraries).

  - Using decentralization revenues to support church-run educational foundations.

  - Redesigning curricula to focus on practical skills, as well as science and math.

- Improving the pedagogy of teachers and increasing compensation for qualified instructors.

- Allowing rural residents to attend primary and secondary education near their homes instead of moving students to the population centers.

- Increasing tertiary and vocational studies.

- Establishing a new university in a city that currently does not have one (e.g., Nabire or Wamena) and developing links between Papuan and other universities.

- Increasing fellowship programs for Papuans to attend international educational institutions.

To improve Papuan health conditions and bring standards into line with conditions elsewhere in Indonesia, the Commission recommends that

- The Indonesian government work with UN agencies and donors to conduct an assessment of the health services sector.

- The Indonesian government work with the World Health Organization (WHO), UNICEF, and donors to overhaul the health system by

  - Raising awareness about health and nutrition through the media, advertising, and education in schools, in local clinics, and via women's groups.

  - Encouraging more Papuans to visit their local clinic, and providing prenatal screening and prenatal and infant health education to pregnant women.

  - Enhancing health services by expanding primary health care and offering HIV/AIDS treatment and awareness programs.

  - Increasing fellowships for Papuans to attend medical and nursing schools outside of Papua.

  - Upgrading the capacity of the Provincial Department of Health and earmarking increased budgetary resources for health from decentralization.

- Establishing hospitals in major urban centers (e.g., Wamena), increasing support for rural clinics *(puskesmas)*, and providing better pay to qualified health-care providers.

- Improving the quality and number of health-care providers by establishing a medical and nursing school.

To improve media and communications in Papua, the Commission recommends that

- USAID increase support for local and regional newspapers in Papua with a focus on balanced news reporting.

- USAID provide additional radio equipment for Internews's four existing newsrooms, and expand InterNews's "Reporting for Peace" radio programs, targeting local ties with a history of ethnic tension, especially Papuan-migrants tension (e.g., in Fak Fak and Manokwari).

- USAID increase the number of InterNews-supported radio stations in Wamena, Manokwari, Fak Fak, Biak, and Nabire.

- USAID coordinate additional internships through InterNews for news staff of Papuan radio stations at news stations in Jakarta or Bandung (e.g., Smart or Mara).

- USAID support the formation of another Internet service provider in the province.

- Donors develop a school of journalism at the University of Cendrawasih (UNCEN) and increase the number of scholarships to national and international universities.

To improve the natural environment of Papua, the Commission recommends that

- The Indonesian government work with UNDP and donors to develop a comprehensive natural-resource management plan for the marine and coastal industries, and a forestry land-use plan.

- The Indonesian government upgrade the Provincial Department of Environment and improve enforcement capabilities of the Environmental Impact Management Agency (BAPEDALDA).

- The Indonesian government develop standards governing industrial water and solid waste, as well as air-pollution control measures, and adopt licensing procedures for the mining and petroleum sectors.

- National and provincial authorities create a mechanism for arbitrating land-use claims and environmental-damage claims by local communities.

JUSTICE AND RECONCILIATION

CONDITIONS

Transitional justice includes strategies for prosecuting perpetrators, uncovering the truth regarding rights violations, reforming abusive institutions, providing reparations to victims, and promoting reconciliation. A successful strategy balances retrospective endeavors, which may seek to document and acknowledge human rights abuse and pursue accountability for past crimes, with prospective initiatives aiming to build institutions that uphold the rule of law and promote genuine reconciliation.

In Papua, post-Suharto reforms raised the hopes of the people of Papua that there would be a general improvement in the human rights situation. The Second Papuan Congress, held in June 2000 and attended by over 25,000 ethnic Papuans from all tribes and communities, rejected the idea that Papuans voluntarily decided to integrate with Indonesia and called for steps to "rectify history" *(meluruskan sejara)*. Stating that the 1969 Act of Free Choice was conducted under circumstances of coercion and intimidation, delegates established the Papua Presidium Council (PDP) to represent the broad Papuan community and advance *merdeka*.[65] During Independence Day celebrations on August 16, 2001, President Megawati Sukarnoputri apologized for past policy mistakes and army excesses in Aceh and Papua. She vowed to abandon the policies of the past, to strengthen the rule of law, and to bring human rights offenders to justice

A strong antiviolence movement has been developing in Papua and has achieved significant success in reducing sectarian and militia-sponsored violence. This movement, which includes leaders of

---

[65] *Merdeka* refers to a utopian concept born from Papuan liberation theory, which represents freedom, independence, and an end to oppression. The term has become associated with a call for an end to Indonesian rule in Papua.

churches, civil-society groups, Papuan and non-Papuan ethnic groups, academics, and the Provincial Police (POLDA) organized a "Peace Conference" in Jayapura (October 2002). This conference resulted in the formation of the Peace Commission for Papua (also called the "Peace Task Force for Papua"). This independent collaborative body works to prevent violence through dialogue, thereby establishing Papua as a "Zone of Peace" *(Zona Damai)*. The Provincial People's Legislative Council (DPRD) has supported this initiative and is passing legislation declaring Papua a "Zone of Peace."

And yet, serious human rights abuse continues to occur in Papua with little accountability. In 2001, political freedoms were curtailed; political leaders were arrested, harassed, and threatened; and peaceful pro-democracy demonstrators were targeted. There are continuing allegations of reprisals against whole communities for incidents involving the Free Papua Movement (OPM). The Institute for Human Rights Study and Advocacy, (ELSHAM), the leading human rights organization in Papua, cites 136 cases of extrajudicial killing and 838 cases of arbitrary detention and torture (1998–2001). Three women, including the wife of Johannes Bonay, executive director of ELSHAM, were injured when their car was fired upon (December 28, 2002). Human rights defenders continue to face serious threats to their lives. In 2001, the UN Special Rapporteur on Violence against Women and the UN Working Group on Arbitrary Detention were denied access to Papua by the national government.

In recent years corporations have been developing community-based security strategies. They have demonstrated a greater commitment to corporate social responsibility and human rights while attempting to overcome the perception that they have turned a blind eye to human rights abuse.

TRENDS

Most people in Papua have little confidence that provincial authorities will take action against members of the security forces who commit crimes. For example, those responsible for the killings in Wamena (1977), the murders of Arnold Ap (1984) and Near-an-Nebelan Anggaibak (1994), the rapes in Mapenduma (1996), and the Biak flag-raising incident (1998) have not been brought to justice. It is striking that no member of the security forces has ever been convicted and appropriately punished for human rights abuse in Papua.

Seven KOPASSUS (Special Forces) members have been convicted by a military court of killing PDP Chairman Theys Eluay. The trial represents an important opportunity for the national government to demonstrate a commitment to accountability. At this writing, there has been no attempt to fix responsibility up the chain of command for the command responsibility—if not the specific orders—that led low-ranking soldiers to physically assault, and kill, this prominent Papuan leader.

In response to a proposal from the governor, the Special Autonomy Law calls for a truth commission to "[stabilize] the unity and integrity of the people of the Papua Province." The objectives of the proposed commission are to "clarify the history of Papua, to stabilize the unity and integrity of the nation within the Unitary State of the Republic of Indonesia," and to "formulate and determine…reconciliation measures." In 2001, President Megawati gave Coordinating Minister for Political Affairs Bambang Yudhoyono the responsibility for beginning a National Dialogue on Reconciliation with pro-*merdeka* leaders in Papua. Though Bambang Yudhoyono has met with leaders of the PDP, the dialogue has stalled.

In 2002, KONTRAS Papua (Commission for Anti-Violence and Forced Disappearance) started a round of meetings with academics, local parliament members, and the media to discuss plans for a Truth and Reconciliation Commission. Participants stressed the importance of broad participation in defining a mandate for the commission.

Report

OPTIMUM SITUATION

A process for addressing human rights abuses and taking into account Papua's violent history is essential to ending conflict and addressing the oppression and distrust felt by many ethnic Papuans. Lack of accountability fosters a vicious cycle of greater rights violations and increased radicalism on the part of ethnic Papuans.

Measures are needed to enhance the entire justice system, from the police to prisons and the courts. Particular attention would be paid to training impartial and professional judges, judicial clerks, and prosecutors. Establishing clear benchmarks, reviewing performance, and dismissing personnel who are incompetent or guilty of corrupt practices would also advance accountability.

Better pay for local officials would help minimize corruption. Dispute-resolution mechanisms would draw on *adat* traditions. Interfaith and women's movements are also pivotal partners in creating a dialogue to account for Papua's violent history and promoting improved intergroup relations. For example, Muhammadiyah, Indonesia's second largest Muslim organization, is sending a delegation to Papua for interfaith discussions.

International experience indicates that truth and reconciliation initiatives are effective only if all parties, but particularly those that have suffered human rights abuse, feel confident that the past will be investigated in an open and independent manner. Efforts to pursue truth and reconciliation will fail if ethnic Papuans feel that an emphasis on national unity is impeding an honest examination of the past. Conversely, the government has much to gain if ethnic Papuans feel that their suffering has been properly acknowledged and if appropriate remedial measures are adopted.

While necessarily led by Indonesian authorities, an effective truth and reconciliation process would be based on a thorough consultation process with NGOs, local communities, and victims in Papua. To be effective, the truth and reconciliation process must not be regarded as a manipulated political process, a substitute for accountability, or a means to grant amnesty for violations of human rights.

RECOMMENDATIONS

To create accountability, the Commission recommends that

- The Indonesian government strengthen the office of the Indonesian National Army (TNI) Inspector General to take up corruption complaints; expand the POLRI Indonesian (National Police) Office of Professional Responsibility; and create Papua branch offices of the TNI Inspector General and the POLRI Office of Professional Responsibility.

- TNI, POLRI, and leaders in Papua establish a mechanism for more effectively investigating and dealing with citizen accusations of security-force misconduct.

- The Indonesian government and authorities in Papua ensure that persons responsible for human rights abuses are prosecuted before impartial courts staffed by independent judges and prosecutors.

- The Indonesian government and the DPRD develop a program to train and properly support an independent judiciary in Papua.

- Donors, international organizations, and businesses operating in Papua provide adequate support to local organizations involved in human rights education and monitoring.

- The Indonesian government allow UN special rapporteurs and international human rights monitors access to Papua.

To advance a truth and reconciliation process, the Commission recommends that

- The Indonesian government, in consultation with Papuan figures such as the governor, DPRD members, and civil-society and religious leaders designate a "Reconciliation Group," led by a prominent individual, to consult with Papuans and international specialists on re-energizing the National Dialogue on Reconciliation and developing an appropriate truth, justice, and reconciliation process for Papua as called for in the Special Autonomy Law.

To advance more harmonious intergroup and inter-religious relations, the Commission recommends that

- Religious, ethnic-based, and tribal organizations continue their dialogue on the peaceful resolution of disputes, and donor resources be used to institutionalize the dialogue through the strengthening of a permanent governing body (e.g., the Papua Peace Commission).

- Provincial authorities strengthen *adat* customary law in combination with due process and human rights safeguards to more effectively manage local disputes and mitigate conflict escalation.

STAKEHOLDER INCENTIVES AND ACTIONS

The section of this report on international stakeholders provided an analysis of stakeholder interests and patterns of stakeholder participation. As part of its "carrots and sticks" approach, the Commission emphasizes the role of stakeholders in providing inducements to influence key national and local actors.

The key to mobilizing international stakeholders is working in cooperation with the Indonesian government and through existing organizations and mechanisms for official development assistance. To this end, the Commission recommends that

- The European Commission (EC) propose and secure support for adoption of a "Preventive Development Program" at the next meeting of the World Bank Consultative Group on Indonesia (CGI).

- The United Nations Development Programme (UNDP) and donor countries conduct a "Preventive Development Assessment" to review existing conflict-prevention activities, identify programming gaps, and develop an overall preventive-development strategy for Papua.

- The CGI draw on its members to establish a "Papua Committee" with donor affinity groups (DAGs) to assist donor coordination and raise new funds for activities developed as part of the Preventive Development Program.

- A donor, such as Japan, host a conference to launch the Preventive Development Program.

KEY COUNTRIES

The Commission recommends that influential stakeholders, such as the United States and other concerned countries, give Papua much greater prominence in their dialogue with Indonesian officials. It is important that stakeholder governments develop a better understanding of the situation in Papua. The Commission believes its report can be used for this purpose. It also urges stakeholder governments to dispatch Jakarta-based embassy officials for regular fact-finding in Papua. Friends of Indonesia should point out to Indonesian officials that a Papuan policy dominated by security concerns will radicalize people in Papua, increase prospects for deadly violence, and fuel international demands for humanitarian action.

Concerned countries can back up this message by providing relevant technical assistance, particularly as it affects Special Autonomy. Donors may also designate grant aid that improves the welfare of the people in Papua by enabling them to realize self-government and a greater share of the province's natural-resource wealth.

The Performance-Oriented Management Program (PERFORM) of the U.S. Agency for International Development (USAID) has been noteworthy for its assistance to district-level administrators and deserves further support. USAID's Legal Reform Program is also meritorious. Programs aimed at strengthening the rule of law would involve institutional development at the national and local levels, as well as prosecution of important Papuan cases, such as the Tembagapura killings (August 2002). The Office of Transitional Initiatives (OTI) could expand quick-impact projects incorporating preventive-development strategies into project design and development. Though donor countries, including Japan, are reducing their budgets for official development assistance (ODA), scarce donor resources can be leveraged through creative mechanisms linking ODA with conflict prevention.

The Commission recommends that UNDP and donor countries conduct a "Preventive Development Assessment," in line with ongoing preventive-development activities in Indonesia, to review existing conflict-prevention activities and identify programming gaps. To raise new grants, DAGs would be chaired by a donor country with expertise in the thematic area.

MULTILATERAL FRAMEWORKS

Precedent exists for linking donor assistance to a domestic peace process in Indonesia. The approach of international funding agencies to the Aceh conflict is instructive. At a donors' conference in Tokyo on December 3, 2002, donor countries and funding agencies pledged to provide substantial funds for postconflict reconstruction, focusing on humanitarian assistance, health, education, and infrastructure.

The same principle could be brought to bear in Papua. But instead of targeting postconflict reconstruction, investments would focus on conflict prevention. Using the United Nations Development Assistance Framework (UNDAF), the United Nations Country Team, in cooperation with donor countries, would conduct a "Preventive Development Assessment." The EC would, as follow-up to its 2001 Conflict Prevention Assessment Mission to Indonesia, propose and secure support for adoption of a "Preventive Development Program" at the next meeting of the CGI. Given the leading role that Japan plays in development efforts in post-conflict situations, the Commission recommends that the government of Japan propose to the CGI that an initial meeting be held to define terms of reference, discuss donor structures and responsibilities, and secure startup financing.

INTERNATIONAL FINANCIAL INSTITUTIONS

Drawing on its members, the CGI would establish a "Papua Committee" with DAGs to assist donor coordination and capitalize on the interest of donors in linking development and conflict prevention by raising new funds. If the EC and other donors are going to increase contributions, they will insist on transparency and accountability. Rather than strict conditionality, donors would adopt an informal monitoring mechanism. The Commission recommends that Papua Committee participants collaborate in evaluating the impact of donor funds and assessing whether contributions have helped realize reforms.

Multinational Corporations

This report discussed the activities of Freeport-McMoRan Copper & Gold Inc. and other multinational corporations doing business in Papua, and made specific recommendations for enhancing their contribution to peace and progress in Papua. Most of these recommendations endorse programs already underway in the areas of local economic assistance, financial transparency, security, and reconciliation. The Commission recommends that these companies continue and intensify their programs to make implementation of Special Autonomy successful. If Freeport and BP act in concert, they can make a real difference.

The Commission believes that international businesses can mitigate conflict escalation by encouraging the Indonesian government to change its approach to projecting security in Papua. It is not in the interest of multinational corporations to contract the Indonesian National Army (TNI) security in the long run. Recognizing the difficulties associated with this arrangement and that it cannot be terminated suddenly, the Commission recommends that international businesses negotiate with the government a plan to gradually remove TNI security. It also recommends that businesses further privatize security functions and incorporate a competent local guard force. Multinational corporations would also provide thorough and regular reports on their compliance with the "Voluntary Principles on Security and Human Rights." The Commission endorses the "Publish What You Pay" initiative of the Open Society Institute.

Nongovernmental Organizations

This report also discussed current activities by nongovernmental organizations (NGOs) in Papua and recommended measures to enhance their efforts. In order to raise greater awareness of progress and problems in Papua, the Commission recommends establishment of a Papua Monitoring Group (PMG), which would monitor conditions and, when helpful, raise Papua's profile in the international community. Made up of local experts among NGOs, the PMG would issue quarterly reports and, when necessary, prepare urgent alerts. Organized by the Center for Strategic and International Studies (CSIS) in Jakarta, the PMG would be co-chaired by Jusuf Wanandi of the CSIS in Jakarta and Barnabus Suebu, the former governor of Irian Jaya. Project finance could be provided by a donor country with special interest in the role of civil society in peace-building (e.g., Norway).

Support is recommended to a qualified international NGO, such as the International Center for Transitional Justice (ICTJ), for activities in Jakarta and Papua that would raise awareness of international models for truth and reconciliation, as well as provide technical assistance toward a strategy appropriate to the situation in Papua.

The "Preventive Development Assessment" would also include an NGO component by considering ways to enhance cooperation between the many secular and religious NGOs conducting social-development programs in Papua.

Dissemination/Policy Coordination

One of the important lessons from last year's Aceh agreement (December 9, 2002) is that the government must take proactive steps to energize a dialogue addressing conflicts on its territory. Designating Ambassador Wiryono, a retired diplomat with experience as a mediator in Mindanao, was essential to focusing government policy on negotiations concerning Aceh. The involvement of Hassan Wirajuda and Coordinating Minister for Political and Security Affairs Susilo Bambang Yudhoyono was also critical to success. So was getting the attention and securing the personal involvement of President Megawati Sukarnoputri.

The Commission recommends convening a meeting to review its report. The meeting would include Papuan representatives, as well as officials participating in the Indonesian government's interagency working group on Papua. The Commission hopes that discussions evolve into an ongoing dialogue.

Report

The Indonesia Commission on Peace and Progress in Papua will not act as a mediator. Its report could serve, however, as a starting point for discussions about promoting trust, building confidence, and enhancing conflict prevention.

APPENDIXES

APPENDIX A: COMMISSION MEMBERS

DENNIS C. BLAIR, the Chairman of the Indonesia Commission, is a Senior Fellow at the Institute for Defense Analyses and an adjunct Senior Fellow in National Security Studies at the Council on Foreign Relations. He is a retired Admiral, United States Navy, and the former Commander-in-Chief of the United States Pacific Command.

PATRICK M. BYRNE is the Chief Executive Officer (CEO) of Overstock.com. He is also the owner of High Plains Investments LLC. Previously, Dr. Byrne was the CEO of Centricut LLC and of Fechheimer Brothers, Inc. He serves on the Advisory Committee of the Center for Preventive Action at the Council on Foreign Relations. Dr. Byrne received his Ph.D. from Stanford University and is a published author.

NAT J. COLLETTA teaches at the Elliot School for International Affairs at George Washington University and has previously taught at other major universities. He was the Founding Manager of the World Bank's postconflict unit and senior spokesperson for the World Bank on reconstruction and peace-building in postconflict societies. He provides advisory services in conflict prevention and postconflict reconstruction to governments, corporations, and the international donor community. Dr. Colletta's career at the World Bank has included secondments with the government of Indonesia and with UNICEF.

RAUF DIWAN is a Managing Director of Emerging Markets Partnership (EMP) and will become CEO of AIG Asian Infrastructure Fund in May 2003. Prior to joining EMP in 1997, Mr. Diwan served for fifteen years with the International Finance Corporation (the World Bank's private equity arm), where in 1997, he was Director of the Global Power Department, and from 1994 to 1995 headed the East Asia Division.

BENNETT FREEMAN is Principal of Sustainable Investment Strategies, a Washington, D.C.–based consultancy advising multinational corporations, international institutions, and NGOs on issues of corporate responsibility, human rights, and international relations. In 2002, he co-authored an independent human rights impact assessment of the BP Tangguh project in Papua, Indonesia, the first such assessment in the world ever undertaken in advance of a major energy project. As U.S. Deputy Assistant Secretary of State for Democracy, Human Rights, and Labor from 1999 to early 2001, Mr. Freeman was the principal architect of the Voluntary Principles on Security and Human Rights, the first human rights standard forged by governments, companies, and NGOs for the extractive sectors.

JOACHIM GFOELLER JR. co-founded GMG's predecessor fund, GMS Capital Partners LP, in 1997 and has served as its Managing General Partner ever since. Prior to joining GMS, Mr. Gfoeller was one of the Founding Partners of Stolberg Partners and served as a Vice President of Weiss, Peck & Greer.

BRIGHAM M. GOLDEN is currently completing a doctoral thesis about PT Freeport Indonesia in the Department of Anthropology at Columbia University. Mr. Golden has spent six of the last eleven years in Indonesia, much of that time in Papua, conducting ethnographic research.

ROBERT F. GREALY is the Director of International Relations Asia-Pacific at J. P. Morgan Chase & Co. Mr. Grealy serves on the Board of Directors of the American Indonesian Chamber of Commerce.

CHARLES GREGORY is Director of Schools Management at International Schools Services, a Princeton-based nonprofit provider of educational services to international schools and multinational corporations. Mr. Gregory has been involved in education since the early 1970s and has been head of international schools in the Middle East, Africa, Southeast Asia, and the Caribbean.

JANINE W. HILL is Associate Director of the Center for Preventive Action at the Council on Foreign Relations.

SIDNEY R. JONES, before joining the International Crisis Group as its Indonesia Project Director, was Executive Director of the Asia Division of Human Rights Watch from 1989 to 2002. An Indonesia specialist with twenty years' experience working in and on that country, she also served as Director of the Human Rights Office of the UN Transitional Administration in East Timor from December 1999 to July 2000.

MARIA J. KRISTENSEN is a Research Associate for the Center for Preventive Action at the Council on Foreign Relations.

JONATHAN E. LEVITSKY is an attorney with the law firm of Debevoise & Plimpton in New York City. He previously served as Counselor to Ambassador Richard C. Holbrooke at the U.S. Mission to the UN, as a Member of the State Department's Policy Planning Staff, and as a Law Clerk to Justice John Paul Stevens of the U.S. Supreme Court.

RANDOLPH MARTIN is the former Senior Director for Operations for the International Rescue Committee and Coordinator for CARDI, a four-member Euro-American NGO consortium providing humanitarian and re-integration programming in Indonesia. Mr. Martin has been involved in international humanitarian operations for over twenty years, including senior management positions in Africa and Asia.

ANN MARIE MURPHY is an Adjunct Professor of Political Science at Barnard College and a Research Scholar at the East Asian Institute of Columbia University. She has managed the Transition Indonesia project, a joint American-Japanese-Australian effort designed to analyze ongoing political and economic events in Indonesia and propose policy options. Her most recent publication is a chapter on Indonesia in *East Asia and Globalization*, and she is currently completing a manuscript on Indonesian foreign policy.

WILLIAM L. NASH is Senior Fellow and Director of the Center for Preventive Action at the Council on Foreign Relations.

MARTIN D. PEATROSS is a Colonel in the U.S. Marine Corps and currently a Military Fellow at the Council on Foreign Relations.

DAVID L. PHILLIPS is a Senior Fellow and Deputy Director of the Center for Preventive Action at the Council on Foreign Relations. In addition, he is Director of the Program on Conflict Resolution and Peace-Building at American University, a Senior Associate at the Center for Strategic and International Studies, Adjunct Professor at the Diplomatic Academy of Vienna, and an analyst for NBC News. Among his previous positions, Mr. Phillips served as a senior adviser to the UN Secretariat and as program director at the International Peace Research Institute, Norway.

JOSEPH SAUNDERS is the Deputy Program Director at Human Rights Watch (HRW). Apart from a brief period as Senior Program Officer at the Carnegie Council on Ethics and International Affairs, he has spent the past six years at HRW. Prior to joining HRW, Mr. Saunders was a Litigation Associate at Cleary, Gottlieb, Steen & Hamilton in New York City and clerked for the Hon. Dorothy W. Nelson of the Ninth Circuit Court of Appeals. Prior to attending law school, Mr. Saunders studied cultural anthropology and spent two years in Indonesia as a Fulbright scholar.

ADAM SCHWARZ is a Consultant with McKinsey & Company and is currently based in Jakarta, Indonesia. Prior to joining McKinsey, Mr. Schwarz ran a political and economic risk consultancy in Washington, D.C., where he also taught at Georgetown University and at Johns Hopkins University's School of Advanced International Studies. Mr. Schwarz spent over ten years in Southeast Asia as a Correspondent for the *Far Eastern Economic Review*. He has authored, edited, or contributed to several books on Indonesia and Southeast Asia, including the highly acclaimed study of contemporary Indonesia, *A Nation in Waiting: Indonesia's Search for Stability*.

CALVIN G. SIMS is a Foreign Correspondent for the *New York Times Television Documentaries* and a visiting professor of journalism at Princeton University. Most recently, Mr. Sims was a Senior Fellow for Asia Studies at the Council on Foreign Relations, where he headed a research project examining the rise of Islamic extremism in Indonesia.

NANCY SODERBERG is Vice President for Multilateral Affairs of the International Crisis Group. Ambassador Soderberg has held high-level posts in the White House, at the UN, and in the U.S. Congress. From 1993 to 1997, she served as the third-ranking official of the National Security Council at the White House, including as Deputy Assistant to the President for National Security Affairs. From 1997 to 2001, she served as U.S. Alternate Representative to the United Nations.

GORDON R. SULLIVAN is the President of the Association of the United States Army and a veteran of the Vietnam War. He was promoted to temporary General in 1990 and served as Army Chief of Staff from 1991 to 1995, when he retired from active service. During his tenure as Army Chief of Staff, General Sullivan presided over fundamental transformations in the Army, overseeing new peace-keeping missions across the globe and leading the Army into the information age.

PAUL VAN ZYL is Director of the Country Programs Unit at the International Center for Transitional Justice and teaches law at the law schools of both Columbia University and New York University. He previously served as Executive Secretary of South Africa's Truth and Reconciliation Commission and as a researcher at the Goldstone Commission in South Africa, and has also been an Associate at Davis Polk & Wardwell in New York City.

APPENDIX B: LOCAL ACTORS IN PAPUA

LOCAL GOVERNMENT

The Provincial People's Legislative Council (DPRD) is the primary legislative body at the provincial level. Headed by John Ibo, the DPRD is currently considering more than 300 regional regulations on Special Autonomy proposed by the Special Regional Regulations Team (Tim Khusus Perda). The Papuan DPRD includes 45 members, 23 of whom are non-Papuan. Ten percent of DPRD seats are allocated to active or retired military officials. The DPRD is responsible for electing Papua's governor and vice governor, *bupati* and vice *bupati*, and mayor and vice mayor, as well as regional representatives to the People's Consultative Assembly (MPR). It also prepares the regional budget and works with the governor, *bupati*, and mayor to develop regional legislation. It implements decrees and regional regulations and supervises the budget and policies of the regional government.

The executive branch is led by the provincial governor, currently Jaap Solossa. The governor is director of all executive offices of the provincial government, which reflect the offices of the central government. The governor is also responsible for the emergency relief system, including assistance to internally displaced persons, and coordinates humanitarian assistance *(bakornas)*. Governors are selected by the central government to serve as the liaison between Jakarta and the provinces.

The Board of National Unity and Community Protection (Badan Kesatuan Bangsa dan Perlindunbgan Masyarakat) is a regional executive department tasked with managing local conflicts and reporting security disturbances to the district head and district police.

The Human Rights Commission in Papua is described in the Special Autonomy Law as a branch of the National Human Rights Commission (Komnas HAM). The law calls for establishment of a Human Rights Tribunal and a Truth and Reconciliation Commission. Local mediation bureaus are also proposed.

The Papua People's Assembly (MRP) is to be established under the Special Autonomy Law as an advisory body of Papuans including *adat* leaders and representatives of religious, women's, and cultural associations. The MRP is designated to advise the DPRD on implementation of the Special Autonomy Law. The MRP is to be regulated by the governor and the DPRD, and election of MRP members will require certification by the Ministry of Home Affairs.

The Village Representative Boards (Badan Perwakilan Desas, or BPDs) include elected members representing different village elements. The BPD has responsibility for resolution of conflicts at the local level.

The Papua *Merdeka* Movement

The West Papua Council is an international umbrella organization of political and guerrilla organizations involved in the struggle for Papua's independence from Indonesia. It was founded as a continuation of the Nieuw Guinea Raad (New Guinea Council), which was originally established on 1 December 1961, and officially approved by the Netherlands.

The Papua Presidium Council (PDP) is a pro-independence political body elected in June 2000 to advance the goals of *merdeka*. The PDP has stood as the single most widely accepted and inclusive body representing the aspirations of ethnic Papuans. After the murder of the PDP's chairman, Theys Eluay, in December 2001, vice-chair Tom Beanal, a widely respected chief of the Amungme tribe and a member of Freeport Indonesia's Board of Commissioners, became the effective leader of the PDP. The Papua Presidium raises funds from a variety of community-based organizations, activist organizations, and corporate interests.

The Papua Panel consists of 501–511 seats, representing individuals and leaders from all tribes, regions, and major social organizations in Papua (including migrants) who are advocating for *merdeka*. The panel convened in May 2000 to constitute the Second Papuan Congress.

The Koteka Tribal Assembly (DEMMAK), established in 1999, is a radical pro-*merdeka* group based in Wamena and closely associated with the Dani tribe, the most populous and influential tribe in the Papuan highlands. The field leader of DEMMAK is Benny Wenda. Sam Karoba is the founder and international chair of DEMMAK. Though DEMMAK is generally supportive of the PDP, it accuses the latter of being too accommodating of the government.

The Mamberamo-Tami Tribal Council (MAMTA) is analogous to DEMMAK, but represents tribal groups in the Mamberamo River and Tami River Territories, including Port Numbay. MAMTA also appears to have links to the OPM/TPN.

The Free Papua Movement (OPM) consists of small and largely uncoordinated guerrilla units that have waged a low-intensity campaign against Indonesian rule since the 1960s. While some OPM leaders reject the PDP's claim to represent all Papuans, the PDP regards the OPM as a component of the Papuan Congress. Though the OPM lacks a coherent organizational structure, most leaders have strong tribal affiliations. Some significant OPM leaders live in exile.

The Papuan National Army (TPN) and the OPM have been perceived as one, but recently the TPN has differentiated itself from the OPM. The TPN was formed when some OPM groups organized themselves into a "Papuan National Army" (Tentara Papua Nasional) and created a Papua-based military wing. The TPN has nine regional commanders, who are largely independent and autonomous.

The OPM Revolutionary Council is a pro-independence political organization founded in the Netherlands in the 1980s and currently based in Madang, Papua New Guinea. This organization makes frequent public declarations but does not have wide support among Papuans, whether inside or outside of Papua.

International supporters of Papua *merdeka* typically take a radical pro-independence stance, including calls for a referendum of self-determination. Efforts are underway to coordinate their activities by establishing the Papua Solidarity Group. Participants include International Action for West Papua, the Oxford Papua Rights Campaign, TAPOL (U.K.), Cultural Survival (U.S.), and the Australian West Papua Association.

Papuan Civil Society

The Papuan Traditional Council (DAP) is a newly formed indigenous decision-making body of tribal leaders. The DAP wields wide-ranging political and moral authority among ethnic Papuans.

Tribal leaders are extremely significant in Papua's political and social landscape and can be found in all ethnic Papuan communities. Major tribes of Papua include: Biakans (Biak), Dani (Wamena and environs), Sentani (Jayapura), Amungme (Tembagapura), Marinir (Merauke), Ekari (Paniai), Moni (Paniai), Asmat (Agats), and Kamoro (Mimika). Tribes of a certain region tend to support each other in provincial-level politics even though they often compete locally.

Protestant churches are a leading social force among Papuans. They provide both spiritual support and essential social services in areas such as education and health. The largest association of Protestant churches is the Indonesian Christian Churches (Gareja Kristian Indonesia, or GKI). The second largest is the GKII, and then the Baptist Church. Smaller Pentecostal and Adventist associations also exist. The Protestant-sponsored Mission Aviation Fellowship (MAF) provides transportation and communication services to communities throughout Papua.

The Catholic Church is a leading social force among Papuans and provides spiritual support and essential social services. The Catholic Church in Papua encompasses four dioceses. Each diocese has a division called "Peace and Justice" that actively advocates Papuan interests. The Diocese of Jayapura is particularly active and has responded to conflict by developing dialogue mechanisms and monitoring human rights conditions. The leader of the Jayapura Diocese division of Peace and Justice is Brother Theo Van der Broek.

The All-Inclusive Papuan Dialogue is an ad hoc process involving a broad cross-section of all Papuans in a dialogue about realizing Papuan interests. It bridges the political divide between pro-independence leaders and Papuans who support existing integration with Indonesia. The All-Inclusive Papuan Dialogue is linked to the National Dialogue on Reconciliation, to which President Megawati has appointed Minister Bambang Yudhoyono.

Nongovernmental organizations (NGOs) in Papua are diverse and wide-ranging. Major NGOs include ELSHAM (the Institute for Human Rights Study and Advocacy, led by John Rumbiak and John Bonay); WALHI-PAPUA & YALI (the Papuan Forum for the Environment, led by Robert Mandosir and Denny Yomaki); the YPMD (the Foundation for the Development of Papuan People, led by Deky Rumaroepen); and the KKW (the Women's Working Group, led by Yusan Yeblo).

The West Papuan Community (WestPaC) is an international network of Papuan academics and students that conducts research and seminars on the political problems of Papua. Papuan academics and intellectuals are important civil-society leaders and role models. They include Benny Giay, Octo Mote, Willy Mandowen, Barnabas Suebu, Feri Karet, and UNCEN (Cendrawasih University) rector Frans Waspakrik.

The Alliance of Papuan Students (Alaiansi Mahasiswa Papua, or AMP International) is a strong pro-independence network that extends to non-Papuan universities. Many of its members are also members of DEMMAK. AMP was established in 1998 by the Communication Forum of Papuan Youth in Jakarta in response to the "Bloody Biak" incident on 6 July 1998. Its main goal is to channel the voice of Papuans to the world, and the message from the world to Papuans.

Group 14 (14 Stars Group) is another name for the Papuan National Party (PARNA), which has been in existence since the 1960s. Its famous leader, Dr. Thom Wainggai, declared Papua a part of Great Melanesia in 1984 and was then arrested and imprisoned for a twenty-year term in Jakarta. He died of food poisoning in early 1996.

The **Melanesian Council** and **Melanesian Solidarity** are linked organizations advocating a pan-Melanesian state.

Independent media include regional newspapers such as *Cendrawasih Pos, Papua Pos, Tifa Papua,* and *Jubi.* National newspapers relatively free of government control are also available, such as *Kompas* and *Suara Pembaruan.*

The Papua Resource Center (PRC), based in New York City, is a nonpolitical organization that seeks to promote Papua's social, economic, and cultural development by facilitating international contacts for individuals and organizations in Papua. Its advisory board includes church, NGO, *adat,* educational, and regional government leaders.

FORERI (Forum for Reconciliation of Irian Society) was established by the leadership of churches, traditional councils, student groups, women's groups, and Papuan NGOs in 1998. It has sought to serve as an independent and nonaligned body mediating the dialogue between the national government and Papuan representatives. The Indonesian government has labeled FORERI a pro-independence group and has blacklisted it.

The Special Committee for Reconciliation is a mediation platform in formation. It includes Papuans of different faiths (i.e., Protestants, Catholics, and Muslims), as well as ethnic Papuans and migrants.

KONTRAS (Commission for Anti-Violence and Forced Disappearance) was formed in March 1998 by a coalition of twelve pro-democracy NGOs including the Independent Committee for Election Watch (KIPP), the Alliance of Independent Journalists (AIJ), the Indonesia Legal Aid Institute Foundation (YLBHI), and the student Indonesian Islamic Student Movement. KONTRAS exists to spotlight disappearances and other abuses in Papua and Aceh.

The Indonesia Legal Aid Institute Foundation (YLBHI) overseas the **Legal Aid** branch in Papua. Legal Aid advocates civil rights and provides legal advocacy with the goal of eliminating social, cultural, and political inequality. It works closely with labor groups, including farmers, fishermen, and the urban poor.

Non-Papuan Militia

Laskar Jihad is a Muslim fundamentalist paramilitary group with strong anti-Western views. Its strong pro-nationalist agenda distinguishes it from other Islamic fundamentalist groups in Indonesia, such as Jemaah Islamiyah. Laskar Jihad forces were agents of sectarian violence in the Malukus, as well as in parts of Sulawesi. Laskar Jihad is increasingly active in Papua, with local bases of operation in the regencies of Jayapura, Fak Fak, Sorong, Timika, Nabire, and Manokwari. In Sorong, Laskar Jihad has established an office under the name of the Communication Forum of Ahlu Sunnah Wal Jamaah (FKAS),[1] which has been active in promoting its *dakwah* (Islamic mission). Despite claims that it had formally disbanded a week before the Bali bombing, there are several indications of continuing Laskar Jihad activity.

Pemuda Pancasila (Pancasila's Youths, or PP) is allegedly involved in illegal businesses (e.g., drugs, prostitution, and extortion) throughout Indonesia. The PP is also linked to atrocities committed in East Timor in 1999. Though the PP appears to be waning in power and numbers, it remains somewhat significant in Papua.

Barisan Merah Putih (Red and White Brigade) is a nationalist militia with a high profile in Papua. It appears to have reduced in numbers but could revitalize its activities in the event of conflict escalation in Papua. Though apparently secularist, the Barisan Merah Putih militia (BMP) appears to have close ties to Laskar Jihad.

The Private Sector

PT Pertamina is the Indonesian state-owned energy company. Pertamina's activities include exploration, production, processing, refining, transportation, and marketing of oil and gas products.

---

[1] Barber, Paul, *Laskar Jihad and Militia Forces in West Papua,* "Letter to Mike O'Brien MP," WPA-UK: 19.

Pertamina works with a number of foreign contractors to develop Indonesia's petroleum resources. Production-sharing contracts and other operating agreements provide the mechanisms for foreign companies to operate in Indonesia. Multinational corporations wishing to enter the oil and gas sector in Indonesia must secure the rights to oil exploration from Pertamina and enter into production-sharing contracts with its regulatory arm, **Badan Pelaksana Migas.**

Indonesian corporations with large operations in Papua include the following:

- PT Jayanti Group (fisheries and wood products), a subsidiary of the Jayanti Group, headquartered in India;
- PT Prabu Alaska (fisheries);
- PT Bukaka Sinetel International (telecommunications);
- PT Korindo (wood products);
- PT Sugino Sari Lestari (fisheries);
- PT Arfak Indra;
- PT Intergalaksi;
- PT Lestari Aneka Sosia Wana;
- PT Baritio Pacific Timber Company (largest plywood and hardwood export company in the world);
- PT Porodisa Group (forestry);
- PT Kayo Lapis Indonesia Group (forestry);
- PT Mutiara Group (forestry);
- PT You Lim Sari (forestry); and
- PT Astra (forestry).

In addition, PT Freeport Indonesia's major national subcontractors include the following:

- Al Latief Corporation (service company);
- Pangansari (service company);
- Airfast (air transport); and
- Trakindo (Caterpillar tractors).

APPENDIX C: THE INDONESIAN GOVERNMENT

EXECUTIVE BRANCH

President
Diah Permata Megawati Setyawati Sukarnoputri

Vice President
Hamzah Haz

Coordinating Ministers
Coordinating Minister for Political and Security Affairs, Susilo Bambang Yudhoyono
Coordinating Minister for Economic Affairs, Prof. Dr. Dorodjatun Kuntjoro Jakti
Coordinating Minister for People's Welfare, Dr. Jusuf Kalla

Ministers
Minister of Home Affairs, Hari Sabarno, M.B.A, M.M.
Minister of Home Affairs and Regional Autonomy, Surjadi Sudirdja
Minister of Foreign Affairs, Dr. Nur Hassan Wirajuda, S.H.,L.L.M.
Minister of Defense, H. Matori Abdul Djalil
Minister of Justice and Human Rights, Prof. Dr. Yusril Ihza Mahendra, S.H., M.Sc.
Minister of Finance, Dr. Boediono
Minister of Energy and Mineral Resources, Dr. Ir. Purnomo Yusgiantoro, M.A., M.Sc.
Minister of Industry and Trade, Rini M.S. Suwandi
Minister of Agriculture, Prof. Dr. Ir. Bungaran Saragih
Minister of Forestry, Dr. Ir. M. Prakosa, Ph.D.
Minister of Transportation, Agum Gumelar
Minister of Marine Affairs and Fisheries, Dr. Ir. Rokhmin Dahuri, M.S.

Minister of Manpower and Transmigration, Jacob Nuwa Wea
Minister of Settlements and Regional Infrastructure, Dr. Ir. Sunarno, Dipl. H.E.
Minister of Health, Dr. Achmad Sujudi, M.P.H.
Minister of National Education, Prof. Dr. H. Abdul Malik Fadjar, M.Sc.
Minister of Social Affairs, H. Bachtiar Chamsyah, S.E.
Minister of Religious Affairs, Prof. Dr. Said Aqiel Munawar

Other (relevant)
State Ministry of the Acceleration of Development in Eastern Indonesia, Dr. Manuel Kaisiepo
Attorney General, Muhamad Abdul Rachman, S.H.
National Intelligence Agency, A. M. Hendropriyono
National Army Commander, General Endriartono Sutarto
Military President Secretary, Brigjen T.N.I. Hasanuddin
President Secretary, Kemal Munawar, S.H.

LEGISLATIVE BRANCH (DPR, MPR)

Post–New Order reformation has been characterized by a strengthening of the legislative system. Recent amendments to the 1945 State Constitution (UUD 1945) have enhanced the People's Consultative Assembly (MPR) and the People's Legislative Council (DPR) and allocated oversight authority over the executive branch. Additional authorities given to the State Audit Board (BPK) and the Supreme Court are intended to establish a clear separation of powers between the legislative, executive, and judiciary branches. Other amendments to the State Constitution limit the maximum tenure for the president and vice president to two five-year terms. Appointments to key positions, such as commander of the armed forces, governor of Bank Indonesia, chief and members of the Supreme Court, and chief and members of the State Audit Board, can be made only with the approval of the DPR.

People's Legislative Council (DPR)

The total number of elected members of the DPR is 500. Of these, 38 seats are presently reserved for the TNI and POLRI. The main roles of the DPR are to prepare a state budget; adopt legislation; and supervise government operations. Akbar Tanjung (Golkar) is the chairperson of the DPR.

DPR Bodies

Headed by the DPR Leadership Group, the Consultative Body represents the DPR in its day-to-day activities during and in between scheduled sessions, sets the legislative agenda, and coordinates activities with the DPR's bodies and commissions.

Other DPR bodies include the Budget Committee, the Internal Affairs Body (BURT), the Inter-Parliamentary Cooperation (BKSAP), the Inter-Parliamentary Organization (IPO), and the ASEAN Inter-Parliamentary Organization (AIPO).

DPR commissions represent the DPR in working meetings with the government (i.e., counterpart ministers), in public hearings with directors-general, or with governmental bodies. Commissions also interface with the business community, and with the directors-general of BUMN (state-owned companies) and BUMD (region-owned companies).

People's Consultative Assembly (MPR)

The total membership of the MPR is 700, consisting of the 500 DPR members, 135 regional representatives, and 65 interest-group representatives. The MPR is assisted by (a) an organizing body, (b) ad hoc committees, and (c) commissions. Chaired by Prof. Dr. H. M. Amin Rais, MA (PAN, Reformasi Faction), the MPR is mandated to

- Sanction the Guidelines of State Policy (GBHN);

- Appoint and/or terminate the president; and

- Amend the 1945 State Constitution.

Regional Government
The provincial government's primary responsibilities are human resources, infrastructure, and economic development, as well as the provision of social services.

Regional Executive Authorities
The provincial governor leads the provincial government's executive branch and coordinates humanitarian assistance (*bakornas*). Under the Special Autonomy Law, provincial governors are elected by the DPRD but answer not only to the legislators and people of the province, but also to the central government in Jakarta. In this sense, the governors are the bridge between the central government and the regencies. There have been recent efforts by the national legislature to empower the governors by giving them increased authority over the regencies.

Provincial Government Departments
Significant provincial government departments include the following:
Department of Social Welfare (Dinas Kesejahteraan Sosial);
Department of Transportation (Dinas Perhubungan);
Department of Trade and Industry (Dinas Perdagangan dan Industri);
Regional Planning Board (BAPPEDA);
Regional Investment Promotion Board (Badan Promosi Investasi Daerah);
Vocational Training Center (Pusat Pelatihan Kerja);
Department of Agriculture (Dinas Pertanian); and
Bureau of Governance Arrangements (Biro Tata Pemerintahan).

The Bupatis
Regional power-sharing under the Special Autonomy Law increases the importance of *bupatis*, or regents for subdistricts within the provinces. As most *bupatis* have links to regional military commands, they often have support from the local military. *Bupatis* are elected by the DPRD.

APPENDIX D:
THE INDONESIAN SECURITY SECTOR

The Indonesian National Army (TNI) has a dual function (*dwi fungsi*): Not only is it responsible for external security, maintaining civil order, and protecting the country's territorial integrity, but since the 1950s, it has played a role promoting social and economic development. The central government provides only 25–30 percent of TNI's budget. TNI raises the balance of its budget through various legal and illegal commercial activities. Though TNI includes Navy (Angkatan Laut) and Air Force (Angkata Udara) departments, the most significant forces are divisions of the Army (Angkatan Darat). These divisions include the following:

- **KOTAMA** (Main Command Forces);

- **KOPASSUS** (Special Forces), a small elite force that operates only in conflict-prone regions;

- **KOSTRAD** (Strategic Reserves Command), typically stationed in conflict-prone regions. KOSTRAD is structured into two infantry divisions, each consisting of infantry brigades. Battalions of approximately 650 men form KOSTRAD's operational and combat units.

- **KODAMs** (Territorial Command Structure), the regional command structures operating in all provinces. The commander of a KODAM is known as the *pangdam*, and the subregional commanders are *dandim*. KODAM personnel constitute the majority of enlisted soldiers in TNI. KODAMs have historically been the backbone of the military's dual function doctrine.

- **TRIKORA**, the special KODAM for Papua.

- **SISKAMLING** (neighborhood security teams), which exist in every village and are nominally part of TNI. Though staffed by civilians, their commander is most often a *babinsa*, usually a sergeant-level officer who lives in the village and acts as local liaison for TNI.

Police duties include internal security, maintenance of the peace, and law enforcement. In April 1999, military and police functions were delineated and their budgets separated. Regional autonomy provisions typically allocate more budgetary and technical responsibility to the police. In Papua, the police have more local recruits and thus tend to command more trust and respect than the TNI. Police divisions include

- **POLRI** (Polisi Republik Indonesia), the Indonesian National Police. Based in Jakarta, it is the agency that technically commands all police forces in Indonesia.

- **POLDA** (Polisi Daerah), the provincial police. Based in each provincial capital, they control and coordinate all the police in a province. The head of a POLDA *(kepolda)* is selected by POLRI.

- **POLSEK**, the local police. They are based in each regency center and control police forces at the local level.

- **GEGANA**, police special forces. Both POLRI and POLDA have special forces units.

- **BRIMOB**, the police mobile brigade. Both POLRI and POLDA have mobile brigade units.

Intelligence units are attached to each TNI and police division. Besides plainclothes and undercover agents, these networks include large numbers of civilian informants (e.g., taxi drivers, hotel employees).

APPENDIX E: LIST OF ACRONYMS

ADB	Asian Development Bank
APEC	Asia-Pacific Economic Cooperation
ASEAN	Association of Southeast Asian Nations
AusAID	Australian Agency for International Development
BAPEDALDA	Environmental Impact Management Agency (Badan Pengendalian Dempak Lingkungan Hidup Daerah)
BCPR	Bureau for Crisis Prevention and Recovery, UNDP
BPD	Village Representative Board (Badan Per-wakilan Desa)
BPMIGAS	Indonesian government petroleum-resource regulator (Badan Pelaksana Migas)
BRIMOB	Mobile Brigade, POLRI
CFR	Council on Foreign Relations
CGI	Consultative Group on Indonesia, The World Bank Group
CIDA	Canadian International Development Agency
CPA	Center for Preventive Action
CSIS	Center for Strategic and International Studies
CSSP	Civil Society Strengthening Program, USAID
DAG	Donor Affinity Group
DAP	Papuan Traditional Council (Dewat Adat Papua)
DPD	Regional Representative Council
DEMMAK	Koteka Tribal Assembly
DFID	Department for International Development, U.K.

DPR	People's Legislative Council (Dewan Perwakilan Rakyat)
DPRD	Provincial People's Legislative Council
E-IMET	Expanded International Military Education and Training Program
EC	European Commission
EITI	Extractive Industries Transparency Initiative
ELSHAM	The Institute for Human Rights Study and Advocacy
EU	European Union
FBI	Federal Bureau of Investigation
FDI	Foreign direct investment
GDP	Gross domestic product
GEGANA	Special Forces, POLRI
GKI/GKII	Indonesian Christian Churches (Gareja Kristian Indonesia)
GOLKAR	Golongan Karya (Functional Groups)
GTZ	German Agency for Technical Cooperation (Deutsche Gesellschaft für Technische Zusammenarbeit GmbH)
HIV/AIDS	Human immunodeficiency virus/Acquired immune deficiency syndrome
HSBC	Hongkong and Shanghai Banking Corporation Ltd.
IBRA	Indonesian Bank Restructuring Agency
ICITAP	International Criminal Investigative Training and Assistance Program
ICRC	International Committee of the Red Cross
ICTJ	International Center for Transitional Justice
IFI	International financial institution
IMET	International Military Education and Training Program
IMF	International Monetary Fund
INPEX	INPEX Corporation
JAPEX	Japan Petroleum Exploration Co., Ltd.
JBIC	Japan Bank for International Cooperation
JEXIM	Japan Export-Import Bank

JICA	Japan International Cooperation Agency
KfW	German Bank for Reconstruction and Development (Kreditanstalt für Wiederaufbau)
KNOC	Korea National Oil Company
KODAM	Territorial Command Structure, TNI
Komnas HAM	National Human Rights Commission
KONTRAS	Commission for Anti-Violence and Forced Disappearance
KOPASSUS	Special Forces, TNI
KOSTRAD	Strategic Reserves Command, TNI
LEMHANAS	National Defense Institute (Lembaga Ketahanan Nasional)
LNG	Liquefied natural gas
MAF	Mission Aviation Fellowship
MAMTA	Mamberamo-Tami Tribal Council
MNC	Multinational corporation
MoU	Memorandum of understanding
MPR	People's Consultative Assembly (Majelis Permusyaworatan Rakyat)
MRP	Papua People's Assembly (Majelis Rakyat Papua)
NGO	Nongovernmental organization
NZAID	New Zealand Agency for International Development
OCPR	Office of Conflict Prevention and Response, USAID
ODA	Official development assistance
OECF	Overseas Economic Cooperation Fund, Japan
OFDA	Office of Foreign Disaster Assistance, USAID
OPM	Free Papua Movement (Organisasi Papua Merdeka)
OSI	Open Society Institute
OTI	Office of Transitional Initiatives, USAID
PDP	Papua Presidium Council (Presidium Dewan)

PERFORM	Performance-Oriented Management Program, USAID
PMG	Papua Monitoring Group
PNG	Papua New Guinea
POLDA	Provincial Police (Kepolisian Daerah)
POLRI	Indonesian National Police (Polisi Republik Indonesia)
PRC	Papua Resource Center
PRIO	Peace Research Institute of Oslo
SIDA	Swedish International Development Agency
TNI	Indonesian National Army (Tentara Nasional Indonesia)
TPN	Papuan National Army (Tentara Papua Nasional)
TRIKORA	Triple Command of the People
U.K.	United Kingdom
UN	United Nations
UNCEN	University of Cendrawasih
UNDAF	United Nations Development Assistance Framework
UNDP	United Nations Development Programme
UNESCO	United Nations Educational, Scientific, and Cultural Organization
UNFPA	United Nations Population Fund
UNICEF	United Nations Children's Fund
UNIFEM	United Nations Development Fund for Women
U.S.	United States
USAID	U.S. Agency for International Development
WHO	World Health Organization
WWF	World Wildlife Fund
YLBHI	Indonesia Legal Aid Institute Foundation

CPA MISSION STATEMENT

The end of the Cold War brought down a world of empires and unleashed a flood of deadly ethnic and civil conflicts; it also set aside major power competition, thus creating the possibility of resolving these deadly local conflicts. The Center for Preventive Action (CPA), founded by the Council on Foreign Relations in 1994, exists to help turn those possibilities into realities by uniting the anti-conflict stakeholders and offering tangible and practical strategies for peace.

In the last decade, this task has proved more desirable than realizable. Yet failing to try to prevent future Rwandas, Bosnias, and East Timors would be a terrible defeat for the human spirit. Nor will it do simply to continue trying and failing. Failure to prevent these horrors will amplify the problems—refugees, starvation, disease, political instability, and declining respect for government—that already plague relations between nations and the daily lives of citizens in conflict-torn areas.

Here's how the CPA will try to prevent deadly conflict caused by civil and ethnic violence, and why we believe we can succeed:

First, we will carefully select countries or regions where prevention has a decent chance, either before killing escalates or in lulls before new explosions. The CPA's Conflict Assessment Forum will draw upon the good analysis that many organizations are already doing, using their early-warning studies to select areas where the CPA can make a difference. We do not intend to waste time redoing already sound work about problems and prospects. Our focus will be to forge agreement on where the CPA can be most useful.

Second, we will establish independent commissions of Council on Foreign Relations members and other experts who understand the roles and views of the outside stakeholders—governments, international organizations, nongovernmental organizations, and the business community—in specific conflict situations. These commissions will develop the necessary strategies (precise recommendations combined with concrete rewards and punishments, carrots and sticks) that could induce key leaders among the warring factions to see new self-interests in altering their behavior to seek a peaceful resolution of their disputes.

Third, we will comprehensively follow through in every way on the recommendations of the commission: prompting congressional hearings, writing op-eds, bringing the appropriate stakeholders and local leaders together in private meetings, and more. The key here is to persevere, and to convince those who can take action that it can be successful—that the strategies offered by the CPA can work, or that the recommended plans can be readily reshaped by the relevant actors to make them work.

These plans, no matter how compelling, will fall on deaf ears unless the CPA can help improve public and government receptivity to conflict prevention. We will have to persuade leaders and citizens that prevention can be an effective and attainable instrument of U.S. foreign policy. This means doing studies, singly or with others, about the role of the U.S. military and its relationship with other government agencies and nongovernmental and international organizations. It means talking with members of Congress about how to meet their concerns regarding open-ended commitments and costs. It means strengthening international organizations. It means showing the business and financial worlds that they have an interest in peace, and that they can play a constructive role in conflict prevention.

CPA ADVISORY COMMITTEE